Modern World Religions

Christianity

Lynne Gibson

Heinemann

Heinemann Educational Publishers
Halley Court, Jordan Hill, Oxford, OX2 8EJ
Part of Harcourt Limited

Heinemann is the registered trademark of
Harcourt Education Limited

Text © Lynne Gibson, 2002

First published in 2002

08 07 06
10 9 8 7 6 5

British Library Cataloguing in Publication Data
A catalogue record for this book is available from the
British Library

10-digit ISBN 0 435 33635 5
13-digit ISBN 978 0 435 33635 6

Picture research by Jennifer Johnson
Typeset by Artistix, Thame, Oxon
Printed and bound in Spain by Edelvives

Acknowledgements
The publishers would like to thank the following for
permission to use photographs:

AKG London/Erich Lessing, p. 14; Andes Press Agency/
Carlos Reyes-Manzo, pp. 10, 11, 18, 24, 25, 26 (right), 30,
34, 36, 44, 46, 51 and 55; The Art Archive/Galleria degli
Uffizi/Dagli Orti, p. 33; Associated Press/Alastair Grant,
pp. 52 and 58 (top); Associated Press/Paras Shah, p. 58
(bottom); Circa Photo Library, pp. 4 (left) and 12; Circa
Photo Library/John Fryer, p. 32; James Davies Travel
Photography, p. 39; Mary Evans Picture Library, pp. 3, 20
and 21; Robert Harding Picture Library, p. 4 (left); Robert
Harding Picture Library/Pearl Bucknall, p. 47; Robert
Harding Picture Library/Jeff Greenberg, p. 54; Robert
Harding Picture Library/David Martyn Hughes, p. 26
(left); Robert Harding Picture Library/ASAP/Garo
Nalbandian, p. 38; Robert Harding Picture Library/Geoff
Renner, p. 40; Robert Harding Picture Library/E Simanor,
p. 40; Impact/John Arthur, p. 35; Panos Pictures/Paul
Smith, p. 42; Science Photo Library/Neil Bromhall, p. 56.

The publishers have made every effort to contact
copyright holders. However, if any material has been
incorrectly acknowledged, the publishers would be
pleased to correct this at the earliest opportunity.

Tel: 01865 888058 www.heinemann.co.uk

Contents

An introduction to Christianity

The word Christos, written in ancient Greek

What is Christianity?

Christianity is one of the major world religions. It has more followers than any other religious tradition. About a third of the world's population, approximately two billion people, are thought to be **Christian**. There are many different kinds of Christians and Christian communities can be found all over the world.

How did Christianity begin and develop?

Map showing the location of Palestine, now known as Israel

Christianity began in Palestine, a country we now call Israel, two thousand years ago. Jesus and his disciples were Jewish. The Christian religion is based on the life and teachings of Jesus. Christianity was the name given to the new religion which was started by Jesus' **disciples** and followers after his death.

The name of the religion comes from the Greek word Christos which means 'the Anointed One'. This was a very special and important title. It referred to someone who was believed to be a saviour sent by God to bring goodness and peace to the Earth. The **Hebrew** word **Messiah** has the same meaning. Jesus' followers began to refer to him as the **Christ** when they believed he had risen from the dead. Their belief in the **resurrection** made them think that Jesus was a saviour sent by God. They became known as Christians, because they were followers of the Christ, the 'Anointed One'.

Christianity has developed in stages. The early Christians were very keen to spread the 'good news' about Jesus. They referred to Jesus as 'good news' because they believed that he was a saviour sent by God. The **apostles**, in particular, travelled throughout the ancient world telling people about Jesus. The early Christians were unpopular with the Romans who ruled large parts of the world at that time. They were persecuted throughout the Roman Empire and sometimes killed for their beliefs. These people were known as **martyrs**.

The first Christian martyr was Stephen who was stoned to death in Jerusalem by an angry crowd. It is estimated that about 40 million Christians in 220 countries have been killed for their faith over the last 2,000 years. At least 100,000 Christians died for their beliefs during the nineteenth and twentieth centuries.

About 300 years after the death of Jesus, the attitude of the Romans towards Christianity began to change. Constantine, a Roman Emperor became a Christian himself. He is said to have seen a large **cross**, the symbol of Christianity, in the sky before he went into battle with his main rival. Constantine won the battle and believed that the God of the Christians had helped him so he converted to Christianity. In 313 CE Constantine passed the Edict of Milan.

This was a law which stated that Christians should be able to follow their religion without being harmed. Very soon after, instead of being persecuted, Christians were given special privileges. Eventually Christianity became the official state religion and spread to the furthest parts of the Roman Empire .

Learning about religion

1. Research how other religions began and developed. Compare and contrast them with Christianity.

2. Find out how many followers other religions have. Present your findings in the form of a graph.

3. Research the life and death of Oscar Romero, Archbishop of El Salvador, and produce a biography of him which explains how his faith influenced his life and why he was martyred. *3 suffer of die fur their believes*

Learning from religion

1. 'Some things are worth risking your life for.' Do you agree? Discuss this statement in pairs.

2. 'Titles are important, they tell us something about a person.' Do you agree? Give reasons for your answer and provide examples to support your statements.

3. Make up your own edict or set of laws setting out what rights you think religious people should have.

A   Constantinus in Anglia natus ibiq, Imperator creatus, uisa Cruce de cœlo audit In hoc Signo Vinces . et Maxentio superato Romam liberat:

B   Idem a Siluestro PP. baptizatur, et a Lepra Sanatur. tum ecclesia templis immunitatibus, et muneribus maximis ornat.

An artist's impression of Constantine at Milvian bridge before he went into battle

Divisions and denominations

In this section you will:

- find out how Christians became divided into different groups
- have the opportunity to reflect upon and express your views about some of the issues raised such as things which need changing in the world today and the responsible use of power.

As Christianity developed, two main centres of power emerged. One group was the Catholic Church which had its headquarters in Rome. The other was the Orthodox Church which was based in Constantinople, now known as Istanbul. In 1054 CE, the Patriarch, the head of the Orthodox Church, accused the **Pope**, the head of the Roman Catholic Church, of **heresy**, having false beliefs.

This was a very serious charge and resulted in the Christian Church being split into two parts: the Roman Catholic Church which is based in Rome and the Orthodox Church which is based in Istanbul. This event is referred to as the **Great Schism**. The Great Schism meant that there were two Christian **Churches** in the world.

During the sixteenth century the Christian Church split into more groups. There were several reasons for this. One reason was that the Roman Catholic Church had become very powerful and many people thought that it was abusing this power. They said that it had forgotten the real message of Jesus and needed to reform or change its practices. In 1517, Martin Luther, a German Priest, nailed a document of protest on the door of Wittenburg Cathedral. The Roman Catholic Church told him to withdraw his remarks and refused to make any changes in the way it operated. Luther was excommunicated which means that he was banned from the Roman Catholic Church. He and his supporters went on to found the Lutheran Churches. For different reasons, similar things happened all over Europe. These events are known as the **Reformation** and led to the founding of four main **Protestant** (from the word protest) Churches: Lutheran, Reformed, Baptist and Anglican.

St Peter's Basilica, Rome and the headquarters of the Orthodox Church in Istanbul

Over time, other people have also become dissatisfied with the Church they belong to. So they have broken away and gone on to form new Churches. The Methodist, Pentecostalist, Salvation Army and Quaker groups have all been formed in this way.

There are many different Christian groups within the Christian Church. Each separate group is called a **denomination**. There are about 25,000 denominations within Christianity. Christians usually belong to a local church which is part of a bigger denomination or Church.

During the seventeenth, eighteenth and nineteenth centuries Christianity was taken to some of the remotest parts of the world by **missionaries**. They travelled to Africa, the Americas, Australia and India and converted people to Christianity.

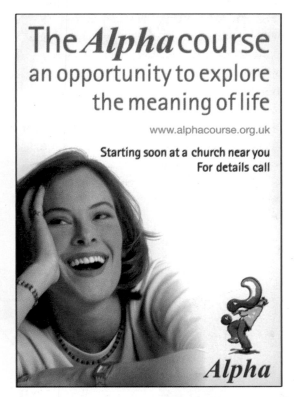

People who are interested in becoming Christians can attend a ten week Alpha Course. Alpha is an evangelical course run by some Churches. It consists of a series of talks which explore the Christian faith. Many people have become Christians after attending the Alpha Course.

Christianity continues to grow and develop today, mainly through the activity of evangelical Christians. Evangelical Christians believe that it is very important to share details of their faith with others. They tell people about Jesus in the hope that they will want to become Christians. Evangelical Christians stress the importance of the Bible and the need to make a personal commitment to Jesus. They have been very successful in attracting young people to Christianity in recent years.

Learning about religion

1. Imagine you have been asked to produce a cover for a book on the development of the Christian faith. The title of the book is *From Twelve to two billion in 2,000 years*. The front cover should be illustrated and the back should contain a written summary which explains the title.

2. Draw a diagram which shows the development of the Christian faith.

3. In groups, research the origins of one Protestant denomination and present your findings to the class.

Learning from religion

1. Write a letter of protest about something you think is wrong.

2. Conduct a survey to see what the members of your class would like to change or reform.

3. Discuss in groups what responsibilities you think a person in a position of power has towards others.

Evidence of Christianity

In this section you will:

- learn how Christianity has influenced the world
- discover how some Christians describe themselves
- have the opportunity to reflect upon what it means to be a Christian and how Christianity might be relevant to your life.

What has Christianity got to do with me?

People who are not religious themselves often think that religion has nothing to do with them. Yet religion can still have an effect our lives even if we are not religious. The diagram below shows some of the ways in which Christianity has influenced the Western world.

Literature

Entertainment

The Calender

Laws

Buildings

Flags

Places

Sport

Jewellery

Vocabulary and speech

Christianity has an impact on...

Business

Name

Charities

The Arts

YMCA/YWCA

Rites of Passage

Carnivals

Food

What is a Christian?

Christians share many common beliefs but they can interpret and practise their faith differently. For example, some Christians have elaborate and energetic forms of worship; others like to keep things simple and prefer to worship in silence. Some Christians choose poverty; others amass great fortunes. Some Christians get involved in political issues in the name of their faith; others believe that religion and politics should be kept separate. Some Christians agree with war in some circumstances; others, called **pacifists**, think that aggression and violence can never be justified. Some Christians accept the use of contraception; others consider it wrong to interfere with nature. Some Christians accept divorce in certain situations; others believe that marriage is forever.

Christians can also have different ideas about what it means to be a Christian. This is what some Christians said when they were asked to describe themselves.

'A Christian is someone who:
…has a personal relationship with God through Jesus
…follows the teachings of Christ
…believes in Jesus Christ
…believes that Jesus is the Son of God
…tries to live their life in the way Jesus wants
…lives according to the teachings of the Christian faith
…has committed themselves to the Christian religion
…belongs to a Church
…has accepted Jesus as their personal saviour
…recognizes that Jesus died to save the world from sin
…has received forgiveness from Jesus
…loves Jesus Christ and their neighbour
…places Jesus at the centre of their lives
…loves and helps their neighbour
…believes in the resurrection of Christ.'

Learning about religion

❶ Prepare a file of evidence which proves that Christianity exists.

❷ 'All the members of a religion should think and act in the same way.' Do you agree with this statement? Give reasons for your answer and provide evidence to support your point of view.

❸ In pairs, imagine you are Christians. Describe your to religion to each other and what being a Christian means to you.

Learning from religion

❶ 'I'm not religious. Christianity has nothing to do with me.' Do you agree with this statement? Give reasons for your answer and provide evidence to support your point of view.

❷ Discuss in groups the different ways we can influence people's lives and evaluate how your actions influence the lives of others.

❸ You are all members of a school. You might also belong to a religion, organization or club. Write a sentence to describe yourself as a follower or member and explain what your association involves.

Sacred writings – the Bible

In this section you will:

● learn about the Bible and find out what the Bible contains

● look at different Christian attitudes towards the contents of the Bible

● have the opportunity to explore the idea of using stories to explain difficult things

● be able to reflect upon what the future might be like.

What is the Bible?

The Bible is the **holy** book of **Christians**. The contents of the Bible are sometimes referred to as **scripture** which means sacred writing. The word 'Bible' comes from a Greek word, 'biblia', which means 'books'. The Bible is often treated as a single book but it is in fact a collection of books. These books are thought to have been written by about 40 different people over several centuries.

What does the Bible contain?

The Bible is divided into two parts – the **Old Testament** and the **New Testament**.

The Old Testament is also the Jewish Bible. Jews refer to it as the **Tenakh**. The Old Testament was first written in Hebrew, the language of the Jews. There are several different versions of the Bible. Most English copies of the Old Testament contain 39 books. They tell the story of the Jewish people and contain a mixture of history, laws, songs, prayers, prophecy, poems and psalms. The Roman Catholic **Church** also accepts another collection books, known as the **Apocrypha**, as part of its scriptures.

The Old Testament		The New Testament		The Apocrypha
Genesis	Ecclesiastes	Matthew	1 Timothy	1 Esdras
Exodus	Song of Songs	Mark	2 Timothy	2 Esdras
Leviticus	Isaiah	Luke	Titus	Tobit
Numbers	Jeremiah	John	Philemon	Judith
Deuteronomy	Lamentations	Acts	Hebrews	Esther
Joshua	Ezekiel	Romans	James	The Wisdom of Solomon
Judges	Daniel	1 Corinthians	1 Peter	Sirach (Ecclesiasticus)
Ruth	Hosea	2 Corinthians	2 Peter	Baruch
1 Samuel	Joel	Galatians	1 John	The Letter of Jeremiah
2 Samuel	Amos	Ephesians	2 John	The song of the three
1 Kings	Obadiah	Philippians	3 John	Young Men
2 Kings	Jonah	Colossians	Jude	Susanna
1 Chronicles	Micah	1 Thessalonians	Revelation	Bel and the Dragon
2 Chronicles	Nahum	2 Thessalonians		The prayer of Manasses
Ezra	Habakkuk			1 Maccabees
Nehemiah	Zephaniah			2 Maccabees
Esther	Haggai			
Job	Zechariah			
Psalms	Malachi			
Proverbs				

How the Christian Bible is made up

The Old Testament is important to Christians because they believe it prepares the world for Jesus. Ancient Jewish prophets predicted that one day a **saviour**, the **Messiah**, would be sent by God to bring peace to the earth. Jesus was a Jew and Christians believe that he was the promised Messiah. Jews disagree with this and say that the Messiah is still to come.

The New Testament was first written in Greek and consists of 27 books. Four of these books tell the story of Jesus and his teachings – Matthew, Mark, Luke and John. They are known as the **Gospels**. The word 'gospel' means 'good news', it comes from an Old English word 'godspell' which means 'message from God'. Christians call these books the Gospels because they believe that Jesus was a saviour sent by God which was 'good news' for the world. The Gospels focus on the last few years of Jesus' life. They concentrate in particular on the last week of Jesus' life, known as **Holy Week**. Most of what we know about Jesus is written in the New Testament. The New Testament also tells the story of the beginnings of the Christian Church and contains prophecies about the future.

Christian attitudes towards the Bible

There are three main attitudes towards the Bible. All Christians believe that the Bible is, in some sense, the Word of God. They believe it tells us about God and what God wants for human beings. Some Christians, called fundamentalists, take this literally. They believe that the words in the Bible have come directly from God. They say that the people who wrote the books of the Bible have accurately recorded, word for word, what God has said. Christian fundamentalists believe that everything in the Bible is true because they say God cannot make mistakes.

Other Christians believe that the Bible is accurate or true to God's Word, however, it does not contain the actual words God spoke.

They say that the writers of the Bible have used their own words to express God's thoughts and ideas.

Another opinion is that the Bible has important symbolic meanings. Some Christians believe that the writers of the Bible have used symbolism to explain what they think God meant. They say that the contents of the Bible may not be completely true because human beings are capable of misunderstanding things and making mistakes.

Learning about religion

❶ Explain why the Old Testament is important to both Christians and Jews.

❷ Read Isaiah 9: 2, 6 and 7 and 11: 1–3. Make a list of the qualities these passages say the Messiah will have. Explain why Christians would want to argue that Jesus was the Messiah prophesized in the Old Testament.

❸ 'You can't believe everything you read in the Bible.' Explain how different Christians might respond to this statement.

Learning from religion

❶ Ask members of your class who or what they would like to write a book about and why.

❷ What would you most like to see happen in the future? Explain what you think the world will be like in the future, or describe your vision of the future.

❸ Think of something that is difficult to explain and make up a story to account for it.

How Christians use the Bible

How do Christians use the Bible?

Christians regard the Bible as an important source of authority. A source of authority is something or someone which tells you what to do. Christians believe that God 'speaks' to them through the Bible. Christians might read the Bible when they have a problem and need help or when they are upset and need comfort.

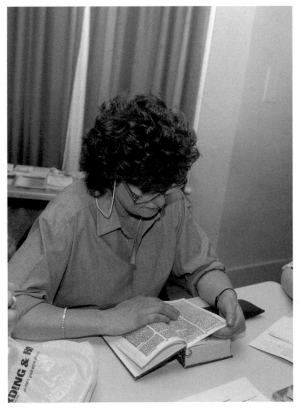

The Bible is a source of inspiration, comfort and guidance for most Christians

Some Christians read the Bible every day as an act of private **devotion**. They may follow a set pattern of readings called a **lectionary**. Christians believe that regularly reading the Bible helps them to find out more about their faith. It also helps them to understand how God wants them to live their lives. Sometimes Christians come together in small groups to study the Bible. They discuss what it says and share what they learn with each other. The Bible is also used during public acts of worship. Passages from the Bible are read out during church services.

The Bible is one of the main ways Christians let other people know about their faith. Christians believe that it is part of their religious duty to tell other people about Jesus. One way they do this is by giving away copies of scripture or by putting them in places where people might be likely to read them.

Gideons International is a Christian organization which places Bibles in hotel rooms, prisons and in doctors', dentists' and solicitors' waiting rooms. They also give **New Testaments** to pupils in schools and put copies of the **Psalms**, a collection of religious songs in the **Old Testament**, and the New Testament, in hospital wards. Many people say that they decided to find out more about Christianity and eventually became a Christian after coming across a Bible this way.

The Bible is an all-time bestseller even though copies are often given away free of charge. More copies of the Bible are sold each year than any other book. The Bible is also available in Braille, on cassette, CD-ROM and the Internet. Some parts of the Bible have been translated into more than 2,200 different languages. The United Bible Society is a non-denominational organization which translates, produces and distributes the Christian Scriptures all over the world. Its aim is to provide copies of scripture in languages people can understand and at prices they can afford.

What do Christians say about the Bible?

'Whenever I have a problem or need help I open the Bible at random and read what it says carefully. I don't know how it works but the bit I read always seems to be relevant.'

'I really enjoy studying the Bible. There is always something new to learn.'

'The Bible is the most amazing book, full of wisdom and wonderful stories!'

'I believe that God 'speaks' to us through the Bible and by reading it we can learn what he expects of us.'
'The Bible tells me about Jesus. It makes him real.'

'I believe that by respecting the Bible I am showing respect to God.'

'The Bible is the key to the past, the present and the future.'

'Reading the Bible makes me feel closer to God.'

Learning about religion

❶ Imagine that you are the head of a company that publishes religious books and you need to justify printing the Bible to your shareholders. Make a list of the reasons why a Christian might buy and read the Bible.

❷ Write two reviews of the Bible, one from a Christian and the other from a non-Christian perspective.

❸ In pairs, role play a Gideon and a member of the United Bible Society having a discussion about the importance of their work.

Learning from religion

❶ Write down a list of your favourite books and explain why you would like others to read them.

❷ What subjects do you enjoy studying the most? Give reasons for your answers.

❸ 'The pen is mightier than the sword.' Discuss in pairs what you think this statement means.

Jesus

In this section you will:

- find out what information Christians have about Jesus
- look at some of the ways Jesus has been represented in Christian art
- have the opportunity to reflect upon important events in your own life
- be able to discuss what you think about the idea of religious experiences.

Who is Jesus?

Jesus is the most important figure in Christianity. His life, death, **resurrection** and teachings form the basis of the Christian religion and faith. Most of what we know about Jesus is found in the **Gospels**, the first four books of the **New Testament**.

What did Jesus look like?

Christians all over the world have produced images of Jesus although no one knows exactly what he looked like

Curriculum Vitae for Jesus

Titles given to Jesus by his followers: Jesus **Christ**, Son of God, The **Messiah**, **Saviour**, Son of Man, Lord.

Titles given to Jesus by his enemies: King of the Jews, Blasphemer, Rebel.

Date of Birth: 6–4 BCE traditionally commemorated on 25 December (Christmas Day).

Place of Birth: Bethlehem, Palestine (now called Israel).

Home Town: Nazareth, Palestine (now called Israel).

Parents: Mary, God and Joseph.

Religion: Jewish.

Occupation: Carpenter and Rabbi (a Jewish teacher).

Hobbies and Interests: Teaching people about God, healing and helping others, storytelling, miracle working, socializing with friends.

Closest Friends: Lazarus, Martha, Mary, Mary Magdalene and the twelve disciples: Simon Peter, John, James, Matthew, Bartholomew, Andrew, Judas Iscariot, Thomas, James, Judas, Simon and Phillip.

Other Associates: The poor, the sick and the outcasts of society.

Significant Moments:

- being taken by Mary and Joseph to Egypt when he was a baby
- being presented in the Temple, the main place of Jewish worship, as a baby
- getting lost on a visit to Jerusalem, the Jewish holy city, with Mary and Joseph and being found three days later in the Temple where he was listening to the Jewish leaders
- being baptized in the River Jordan by his cousin John the Baptist shortly before he began his ministry

- his first miracle: turning water into wine at a wedding in Cana

- his triumphant entry into Jerusalem riding on a donkey (traditionally commemorated on **Palm Sunday**)

- weeping over the state of Jerusalem

- overturning the merchants' tables in the Temple

- sharing a final meal with his disciples (now known as the **Last Supper** where he asked them to eat bread and drink wine in his memory)

- standing trial and being sentenced to death by Pontius Pilate, the Roman Governor

- death by crucifixion

- overcoming death (the Resurrection, traditionally commemorated on **Easter Day**)

- ascending to heaven to be with God (known as the **Ascension**).

Special Achievements:

- surviving forty days and nights in the desert and resisting temptation from the Devil

- healing the sick and crippled

- restoring the sight of the blind

- raising Lazarus from the dead

- feeding 5,000 people with two loaves of bread and five fishes

- walking on water

- calming a storm

- overcoming death (the Resurrection, traditionally commemorated on Easter Day)

- saving the world from sin (**Redemption**)

- repairing the relationship between God and human beings (**Reconciliation**).

Date, time and place of death: In Jerusalem on the Friday before **Pesach** 30–3 CE.

Means of death: Crucified by the Romans at the request of the Jewish religious leaders who accused him of **blasphemy**.

Where do Christians believe Jesus is today?

Christians believe that Jesus is 'alive'. They say that Jesus is in Heaven with God the Father and his spirit, known as the **Holy Spirit**, is active in the world today. Some Christians claim to have met or felt the presence of the 'risen' or resurrected Jesus. Most of these Christians also say that these encounters have changed their lives dramatically. This kind of occurrence is known as a religious experience. Religious experiences can take many forms but they are all events in which people believe that they have in some way come very close to God.

Learning about religion

❶ Prepare a 'This was your life' presentation for Jesus.

❷ Produce a modern symbolic representation of Jesus.

❸ Discuss in pairs why you think there are many different images of Jesus.

Learning from religion

❶ Write your own CV or autobiography.

❷ Describe your most significant moment or special achievement and explain why it was important to you.

❸ 'Religious experiences are just the product of an over active imagination.' What do you think? Discuss this statement in groups.

The early Christian leaders

Peter

One of Jesus' disciples, Peter, went on to become the most important leader of the early **Christian Church**. Again, most of what we know about him is found in the **New Testament**.

Jesus changed Peter's name from Simon to Peter.

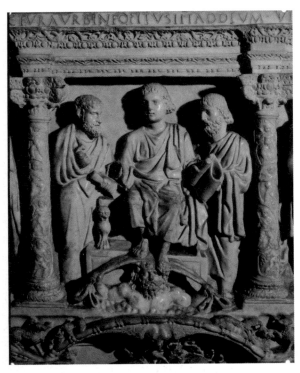

A early Christian sculpture showing Jesus (centre) with the apostles Peter and Paul

The name Peter comes from the Greek word 'petros', which means rock. Jesus told Peter that he would be the 'rock' upon which he would build his Church.

And so I tell you Peter: you are a rock, and on this rock foundation I will build my church, and not even death will be able to overcome it.

Matthew 16: 13–20

After Jesus' death, Peter taught and led the early Jewish Christians. He also went on long missionary journeys around Asia. The New Testament contains two letters (**epistles**) he wrote to the Christian Churches there. Peter, like many of the early Christians, was persecuted, imprisoned and eventually died for his beliefs. He was crucified in Rome, probably sometime during 67 CE. Peter chose to be crucified upside down as a sign of respect to Jesus.

Peter is regarded as the first **Pope** of the Roman Catholic Church and is a **saint** of the Christian Church. St Peter's Basilica in Rome was built in honour of him and has a **shrine** containing his remains. Millions of Christians visit it every year. It is the most popular shrine in the Western world. Peter's special status is often symbolized by him being placed next to Jesus in paintings, carvings and sculptures.

Christians are encouraged by Peter's story. This is because he is seen to make many mistakes yet he is still chosen by Jesus to look after and lead his followers. One of the things Peter did was to deny knowing Jesus three times before the crucifixion.

Paul

The New Testament also tells the story of Paul, another very important figure in the development of Christianity. Paul is sometimes referred to as an apostle even though he was not one of the original twelve disciples.

This is because many people think that Paul, more than any other person, was responsible for turning Christianity into a religion.

Paul, originally called Saul, was Jewish and a Roman citizen. He went to Jerusalem to study and became a well-known persecutor of Christians. Paul is said to have been responsible for the death of Stephen, the first Christian martyr.

One day whilst on the road to Damascus, Paul had an experience which was to dramatically change his life.

As Saul was coming near the city of Damascus, suddenly a light from the sky flashed round him. He fell to the ground and heard a voice saying to him, 'Saul, Saul! Why do you persecute me?'

'Who are you, Lord?' he asked.

'I am Jesus, whom you persecute,' the voice said. 'But get up and go into the city where you will be told what to do.'

The men who were travelling with Saul had stopped, not saying a word; they heard the voice but could not see anyone. Saul got up from the ground and opened his eyes, but could not see a thing. So they took him by the hand and led him into Damascus. For three days he was not able to see, and during that time he did not eat or drink anything.

Acts 9: 3–9

Then a Christian called Ananias visited him and cured his blindness.

Paul was convinced that he had encountered the risen Jesus. He stopped persecuting Christians and converted to Christianity. Paul then spent several years in the desert praying and meditating before going on to be the greatest missionary in the history of the Christian Church. Paul believed that the 'good news' about Jesus was for everyone to hear. He travelled around the Roman Empire preaching to Gentiles (non-Jews) as well as Jews and founded many new Christian churches.

Paul wrote epistles (letters) to these new Christian communities offering encouragement and guidance. His epistles are in the New Testament and provide a lot of information about the early Christian Church. No one knows for sure what happened to Paul. Historians think that he was martyred for his beliefs and probably killed by Nero, a Roman Emperor, in 64 CE.

Like Peter, Paul is a saint of the Christian Church. His special status is also often symbolized by him being placed next to Jesus in paintings, carvings and sculptures.

Learning about religion

❶ Design two symbols to represent Peter and Paul and describe their role in the development of the early Christian Church.

❷ Explain what you think the lives of Peter and Paul can tell us about the Christian attitude towards forgiveness.

❸ 'Peter and Paul are yesterday's news. They don't mean anything to Christians today.' Do you agree? Discuss this statement in pairs.

Learning from religion

❶ Why do you think Paul needed time alone in the desert after his conversion experience? Make a list of the reasons why people might need time to think and reflect and produce a leaflet on the importance of reflection.

❷ Have you ever changed your mind about something important? Write an account of what happened.

❸ Write your own letter or epistle offering encouragement and guidance to someone who is starting a new a venture.

Leaders of the Christian Church

In this section you will:

- find out how three of the main Christian Churches are organized
- look at the role of the **priest** within the community
- have the opportunity to explain how your school is organized and describe your ideal job.

The **Christian** faith is divided into many different **denominations**. The table below describes how the three main Christian **Churches** are organized.

Today, most Christians belong to one of the three main denominations: Anglican, Orthodox and Roman Catholic. These churches all have a hierarchical structure which means that there are various levels of authority. Another similarity is that they all have a ministry of bishops. Churches which have a ministry of bishops are known as **episcopal** (taken from a Greek word which means bishop).

Name of Church	The Protestant Churches	The Roman Catholic Church	The Orthodox Churches
Divisions within the Church	The Protestant Churches include all the denominations which developed as a result of the **Reformation**. In England, the main denomination is the Church of England (Anglican).	There are no separate branches of the Roman Catholic Church.	The Orthodox Church is made up of fifteen national or regional Churches.
Leaders and followers	Members of the Church of England are known as Anglicans. Their way of understanding and following the Christian faith is one form of Protestantism. Each Protestant denomination has its own organizational structure and some involve the ordinary members of the **congregation (laity)** more than others. The Queen is, officially, the head or 'Supreme Governor' of the Church of England. Under the Queen are two Archbishops (senior bishops). Each archbishop is responsible for a particular part of the country. Under the archbishops there are bishops who oversee the running of several churches within a large area called dioceses. Archdeacons rank just below bishops and help them carry out their duties. In each diocese there are priests (vicars) who are responsible for a specific parish or local community within the diocese. Priests are often helped by deacons, people who are training to be priests.	Members of the Roman Catholic Church are known as Roman Catholics. Their way of understanding and following the Christian faith is called Catholicism. The Roman Catholic Church has one leader called the **Pope**. The Pope is elected by cardinals. Under the cardinals there are bishops who oversee the running of several churches within a large area. These areas are called dioceses. In each diocese there are priests who are responsible for a specific parish or local community within the diocese. Priests are often helped by deacons, people who are training to be priests.	Members of an Orthodox Church are known as **Orthodox** Christians. Their way of understanding and following the Christian faith is called Orthodoxy. Each Orthodox Church is independent and has a leader called a Patriarch which means 'great father'. Under each Patriarch there are bishops who oversee the running of several churches within a large area. These areas are called dioceses. In each diocese there are priests who are responsible for a specific parish or local community within the diocese. Priests are often helped by deacons, people who are training to be priests.
Women priests	Several Protestant Churches allow women to become priests. The Church of England has allowed women priests since 1994.	The Roman Catholic Church does not allow women to become priests.	The Orthodox Church does not allow women to become priests.
Religious orders	The three main demoninations each have monks and nuns, groups of men and women who take vows of poverty, chastity and obedience, and dedicate their lives to serving God. Many live a life of service in the community, but some belong to 'enclosed' or 'separate' orders. This means they have very little contact with the community or outside world.		

The role of the priest within the community

Priests often have many roles within the community. One of the main duties of a priest is to look after the spiritual welfare of the people who live in their parish, the geographical area associated with the church. This means that they are responsible for teaching people about God and helping and encouraging them to live their lives according to the teachings of the Christian religion. Christians believe that priests are authorized to forgive people their sins in the name of God. They can lead the community in prayer and worship, celebrate **Holy Communion**, baptize people and prepare them for confirmation and marriage, perform marriage ceremonies and conduct funerals. Christians believe that priests also have an obligation to look after the emotional and physical welfare of the people who live in their parish. This might involve counselling the sick, lonely or depressed and visiting the elderly or people in prison. Other activities of a priest could include running youth groups, visiting schools, meeting with other church leaders, and contributing to the work of the Church in the world. A priest must also find time for personal **prayer** and reflection.

Learning about religion

❶ Compare and contrast how the three main Christian Churches are organized.

❷ Make a list of the reasons someone might want to talk to a priest and explain how a priest might respond in each situation.

❸ Imagine you are a Christian priest in a busy parish. Explain to a partner why it is important for to find time for personal prayer and reflection.

Learning from religion

❶ Draw a diagram to show how your school is organized. Explain the role of each person and the contribution the school makes to the local community.

❷ Describe your ideal job and explain why you would like to do it.

❸ 'You should lead by example.' Discuss in pairs what you think this statement means.

'A day in the life of an Anglican priest'

9.00am–9.30am Morning Prayer service.

9.30am–10.00am Personal prayer and reflection.

10.00am–11.00am Mid-week Holy Communion service.

11.00am–11.30am Coffee with church youth worker.

11.30am–1.00pm Hospital visit.

2.00pm–3.30pm School assembly and meeting with teachers.

4.00pm–5.00pm Bereavement counselling and funeral planning. A home visit to offer comfort to a grieving family and help plan a funeral.

6.30pm–7.30pm **Confirmation** preparation class.

8.00pm–8.30pm Administration, paper work, and preparation for the next day.

8.30pm–9.00pm Read through the agenda for the next Council for Emissions Society meeting.

9.00pm–9.30pm Personal prayer and reflection.

What do Christians believe?

In this section you will:

- study a Christian statement of belief called the Apostles' Creed

- find out what Christians believe to be true about God, Jesus, the world and life after death

- have the opportunity to reflect upon your own beliefs and consider the value of formal statements of belief.

Infant baptism is the ceremony by which babies and children are welcomed into the Christian church

The early **Christians** had many different ideas about their religion, including the identity of Jesus. There were lots of disagreements. Christian leaders thought it was important that everyone knew and agreed upon the basics of the Christian faith. So, during the fourth century CE, two **creeds** (statements of belief) were produced. The word 'creed' comes from the Latin word 'credo' which means 'I believe'. One of these creeds was called the **Apostles'** Creed. It is called the Apostles' Creed because it summarizes the teachings of the apostles, the original twelve **disciples** of Jesus, and sets out the main Christian beliefs.

The Apostles' Creed is an **ecumenical** symbol of the Christian faith. This means that it represents the beliefs of most Christians no matter what denomination they belong to. Anglican and Roman Catholic Churches use the Apostles' Creed regularly during daily prayer and worship. The Apostles' Creed is also a symbol of infant baptism. It describes the faith into which the person being baptized is entering. Sponsors say the Creed during an **infant baptism** ceremony. A sponsor, also known as a godparent, is someone who makes vows on behalf of the person being baptized and promises to help bring them up in the Christian faith.

[handwritten: This sums up the belief in Christianity]

The Apostles' Creed

I believe in God, the Father almighty,
creator of heaven and earth.
I believe in Jesus **Christ**, God's only Son, our Lord.
He was conceived by the **Holy Spirit**
and born of the **Virgin Mary**.
He suffered under Pontius Pilate,
was crucified, died, and was buried.
He descended to the dead.
On the third day he rose again.
He ascended into heaven,
and is seated at the right hand of the Father.
He will come again to judge the living and the dead.
I believe in the Holy Spirit,
the holy catholic Church,
the communion of saints,
the forgiveness of sins,
the **resurrection** of the body,
and the life everlasting. Amen.

[handwritten: rose up to heaven after he died]

[handwritten: Jesus side when gone to heaven.]

[handwritten: all rise again.]

What does the Apostle's Creed reveal about Christian beliefs?

Christians believe that there is one God who has made Himself known to the world in three ways:

Father, Son and Holy Spirit. This does not mean that Christians believe there are three gods. Christians believe that there are three persons in the one God: God the Father, God the Son and God the Holy Spirit. The belief that there are three persons within one God is called the **Trinity**. It is a very important Christian belief. The word 'trinity' comes from the word 'tri-unity' which means three-in-one.

Christians agree that the way the Trinity works is mysterious and difficult to explain. They believe that each person of the Trinity performs a special function: God as the Father created Heaven and Earth, God as the Son is the **saviour** of the world and God as Holy Spirit is an invisible power which guides and inspires human beings.

Christians believe that Jesus is the Son of God, sent to earth by God to save the world from **sin**. They believe that Jesus' death made up or atoned for everything human beings had done wrong since they were first created by God. Jesus redeemed (freed) human beings from sin by his death on the **cross**. This meant that human beings were no longer separated from God by their sins (wrong doings). Christians believe that Jesus made it possible for human beings to have a personal relationship with God.

Christians believe that Jesus was both fully human and **divine**. They believe that God became a man in Jesus. This mystery is known as the **Incarnation**.

Christians believe that Jesus was crucified and died. They believe that he overcame death and rose from the dead three days after he was crucified. This is the central belief of Christianity and known as the Resurrection.

Christians believe that Jesus left the earth forty days after his resurrection. They believe that he ascended (went up) into the presence of God where he occupies a place of honour. The state of being with God after death is known as Heaven.

Christians believe that Jesus will return to Earth one day to judge people and decide who should go to Heaven. This belief is known as the **Second Coming**. It is called the Second Coming because it will be the second time Jesus has come to earth.

Christians believe that faithful Christians, like the early Christian **martyrs** and **saints**, are now in the presence of God.

Christians believe that they are part of a wider Christian community which includes many different Churches.

Christians believe that God forgives the sins of human beings if they repent. This means that they are truly sorry for what they have done wrong. **Forgiveness** and **repentance** are important themes in Christianity.

Christians believe that there is life after death. The idea of **eternal life** is very important to Christians.

Learning about religion

❶ Produce a glossary of the key terms and words used in this section.

❷ Design a symbol to represent the Trinity and describe the main role of each member.

❸ Using a mind map or flow chart, show how Christian beliefs might affect the way Christians live their daily lives.

Learning from religion

❶ What things do you value and believe to be true about life and the world in which you live? Write, explain and illustrate your own creed.

❷ Do you have to understand something to believe it? Is there a difference between belief and faith? Discuss these questions in groups.

❸ 'People are individuals. They shouldn't be told what to believe.' Do you agree with this statement? Give reasons for your answer and provide evidence to support your viewpoint.

Sources of Christian belief

In this section you will:

● investigate the various sources of Christian belief

● discover how some Christians believe God has revealed Him or Herself to them and the impact this has had on their lives

● have the opportunity to reflect upon some of the issues raised such as amazing experiences and optimism.

Christians base their beliefs on what they believe to be true about God and His or Her plans for the world. They believe that God has made Him or Herself known to human beings in a variety of ways. The idea of self-disclosure or God making Him or Herself known to human beings is called **revelation**. There are various sources of revelation in Christianity.

Christians believe the Incarnation is one of the main ways God has revealed Him or Herself to human beings. Jesus' life, death and **resurrection** are a source of revelation and inspiration for all Christians. They believe that Jesus taught them a lot about God and how God wants human beings to live, and His or Her plans for them.

Christians believe that the **Holy Spirit** and the Bible are also sources of revelation and inspiration. Some Christians, known as Charismatic Christians, believe that God, the Holy Spirit, moves people to freely express their joy and delight about their faith. This might include clapping, raising their hands in the air or singing and praying in a special language known as tongues.

Christians believe that the Bible tells them a lot about God, life and the way to **salvation**.

Sports professional Jonathan Edwards claims:

'The Bible is God's word to me, to all of us, to what my attitudes, my actions and the way I live my life should be. Its God's primary way of speaking to me. From the Bible I take the basic philosophy of what I try to do – to glorify God through every aspect of my life'.

Another idea is revelation received through personal experience of God. Many Christians claim to have encountered God through dreams and visions. They believe that these experiences have helped them to understand what God is like and how God expects human beings to live.

Julian of Norwich

During the middle ages a woman known only as Julian of Norwich claimed to have had a series of sixteen visions in which God's love was revealed to her. Julian of Norwich was an anchoress. An anchoress was someone who had taken a vow to live in solitary confinement and devote themselves to prayer and meditation.

Julian of Norwich lived in a cell, or small room, adjoining a church

They were usually confined to a cell or small room adjoining a church. Julian is believed to have seen her visions whilst she was very ill and near death. She recovered from her illness and went on to write two books about her experiences called *Revelations of Divine Love*.

Julian surprised people by repeatedly referring to God and Jesus as 'Mother'. This was very unusual as most Christians then thought that God was male and referred to Him as 'Father'. Julian is also remembered for her optimism. Her visions enabled her to claim, 'All shall be well, and all shall be well, and all manner of things shall be well'.

St Francis of Assisi

Francis of Assisi was born in Italy during the twelfth century. He claimed to have experienced several personal revelations of God which changed the course of his life.

Francis is the patron saint of ecologists, people who study the relationships between animals and their environment. He is said to have developed extraordinary relationships with animals.

One day Francis came across a leper and despite being repelled by what he saw, Francis jumped down and kissed the leper's hand. The leper kissed him back and Francis felt a great sense of joy. A few moments later, the leper was nowhere to be seen. Francis was convinced that he had been tested by God and passed. Shortly afterwards, he had another experience. Whilst praying in an old dilapidated church in front of a crucifix, he heard Jesus speak to him, 'Francis repair my church'. Francis rebuilt the ancient church and went on to found a religious order, a community of monks who followed very strictly the way of life Jesus demonstrated in the Bible.

Learning about religion

❶ Explain what Christians mean by the idea of revelation and draw a diagram showing the different ways Christians claim to know God.

❷ In groups, write and act out a play about a Christian, an atheist (someone who doesn't believe in God) and an agnostic (someone who doesn't know whether God exists), discussing the existence of God.

❸ Discuss in pairs what you think Christians can learn about God from the experiences of Julian of Norwich and St Francis of Assisi.

Learning from religion

❶ 'People who are religious are more likely to be optimistic than pessimistic.' Do you agree?

❷ Have you ever discovered or seen something amazing? Write about your experience.

❸ Create a collage or painting based on the theme 'religious visions and dreams'.

Symbols of the Christian faith

The cross and crucifix

The **cross** is the main symbol of Christianity. The cross can be found in various forms and can have different meanings. For example it can stand for sacrifice, **salvation** and **reconciliation**. But the cross mainly represents the Christian belief in the **resurrection** – the idea that Jesus overcame death and rose from the dead. **Christians** believe that this means there is life after death.

The cross can be used as a sign as well as a symbol. On maps it shows where a church can be found.

The crucifix is a particular kind of cross. It has an image of the crucified Jesus on it. This symbol focuses on the suffering and death of Jesus. It reminds Christians of the sacrifice he made. Christians believe that Jesus died so that human beings could be forgiven their sins and enjoy a new relationship with God.

Bread and wine

The symbols of bread and red wine are used to represent Jesus' body and blood. The **Gospels** that before Jesus died he shared a meal with his **disciples** now known as the **Last Supper**. Here he asked his followers to break and eat bread and drink wine together in memory of him. Eating bread and drinking wine has become an important part of some Christian worship since this time.

Then Jesus took a cup … and said, 'Take this and share it among yourselves …' Then he took a piece of bread … broke it, and gave it to them, saying, 'This is my body which is given for you. Do this in memory of me.'

Luke 22: 17–19

Water

Every living thing needs water to survive and it is often seen as a symbol of life. Some Christians use water as a symbol because they believe that Jesus offered people the opportunity of a new life with God. Water is used in a symbolic way during **baptism**. It represents spiritual cleansing, the idea of washing away sins and starting again.

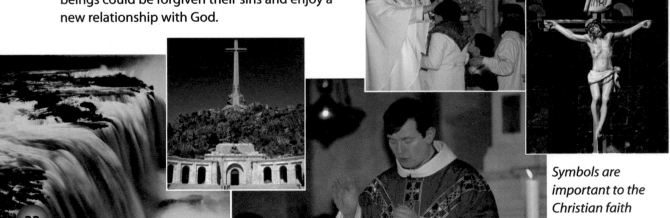

Symbols are important to the Christian faith

Oil

Some Christians use oil as a symbol of healing because, like ointment, it can be rubbed into cuts and burns to make them better. It represents spiritual power. Christians are sometimes **anointed** with **consecrated** oil when they are sick in the hope that God will heal them. They might also have oil put on them during **confirmation** or **chrismation**. This shows that the wounds caused by wrong thoughts or actions are healed. They can put the past behind them and make a fresh start.

In the past important and powerful people like kings were anointed with oil. Oil is seen as a sign of Jesus' kingship: his power and ability to rule over the world. It is still used during some coronation ceremonies.

Some Christian thoughts today

'To me the cross is the most important symbol. It points the way to heaven and reminds me that there is life after death.'

'When I take the bread and wine it reminds me of the sacrifice Jesus made. I feel humble and privileged that God cares so much about us. This act of worship gives me a sense of fellowship and community with other Christians.'

'I was baptized when I was an adult. During the service I was immersed in a pool of water. Before becoming a Christian I had not led a particularly good life. When I came out of the water I felt that everything I had done wrong in the past had been washed away. I knew that God had forgiven me.'

'Fifteen years ago I was very ill and given only six months to live. I was anointed with oil during a healing service. I see oil as a symbol of God's love and His power and ability to help and heal us.'

Learning about religion

❶ Write an article for an **interfaith** magazine explaining what Christian symbols tell us about their understanding of God.

❷ Imagine that you are presenting a radio programme on symbolism. Write an account of an interview between you and a Christian about the main symbols they use and what they mean to them.

❸ 'Christians only use symbols so that they don't have to explain things in detail.' Do you agree? Discuss this statement in groups or with a partner.

Learning from religion

❶ Imagine that you have been asked to commission a symbolic painting which reflects what young people today think about God. Ask members of your class how they would symbolize God. Prepare a set of instructions and sketches for the artist explaining what kind of pictures they would need to paint and why.

❷ Make a list of some circumstances where you might need to make a fresh start. Design symbols to represent them and explain your ideas.

❸ Imagine that you have to go away and leave your friends for a while. Describe what symbolic action you would ask them to do in memory of you. Explain your choice.

How Christians use symbols

In this section you will:

● find out more about Christian symbols

● look at some of the ways Christians use symbols to express their religious feelings, beliefs and ideas

● have the opportunity to evaluate the use of symbols and explore the role of symbolism in your life.

Christians use symbolism in a variety of ways. They have different views about the value of using symbols in their religion. Some denominations deliberately keep symbolism to a minimum because they think that symbols can distract people and take their attention away from God. Other Christian groups believe that symbols can help people to focus on God and they have an important role to play in their faith. Symbolism affects the shape of **church** buildings and the objects inside. It affects the way people worship and how they dress for religious purposes. It also affects the language they use and the way they describe God.

Some churches have been built in the shape of a **cross**, the main symbol of Christianity. Symbols can be an important part of worship. Some churches burn **incense** during their services.

Some churches, such as the Greek Orthodox Church, burn incense during their services

This creates atmosphere and the rising smoke represents prayers ascending to God. Churches are often decorated with flowers. This shows that God is special and they are symbols of love and devotion. Worshippers also light candles. The candle as a source of light symbolizes goodness, knowledge and truth.

Christians call Jesus the 'Light of the World' because they believe that he overcame the darkness of ignorance and evil and showed people the right way to live. Christians often use non-literal or symbolic language to describe Jesus or God. They do this because they believe that it is very difficult to say exactly what God is like so they use symbolism to express their ideas and beliefs about God. For example, Christians often refer to God as 'Father'. They don't literally believe that God is their father but they do believe that He behaves like a caring father towards them.

The way Christians act during worship can be symbolic. Some Christians bend their right knee and bow when they pass in front of the altar, as they enter or leave the church. This is called **genuflection** and symbolizes respect for God. The positions Christians adopt whilst praying are also symbolic. Kneeling down and the bowing of heads whilst praying are symbols of **humility**. The worshipper is acknowledging that God is much greater than they are. Likewise, standing up to pray shows respect. Sometimes Christians prostrate or lay themselves on the ground whilst praying. This gesture shows that they are submitting to or prepared to follow the will of God. It also symbolizes their belief that they are dependent or reliant on God.

During some services, as a symbol of peace, Christians put their arms around each other or shake hands. At other times, the **priest** places their hands on a person's head or body as a symbol of God's blessing and healing. This action is known as the 'laying on of hands'.

Members of the Salvation Army

The colour of **vestments**, special clothes worn by priests during worship, and soft church furnishings like the altar frontals, a decorative hanging in front of the altar, are symbolic and are changed throughout the course of a year. Colour is also associated with certain services and ceremonies. People being baptized, confirmed and a Christian bride traditionally wears white which symbolizes purity. Similarly, the mourners at a funeral sometimes wear black or dark clothing to symbolize their sadness and grief.

Clothing can also have symbolic meaning. For example, a **priest** will wear a clerical collar, usually called a 'dog collar'. The collar resembles the iron halters which were fixed around the necks of slaves. It symbolizes that priests are not their own master but do the work of God. Monks and nuns, Christians who belong to religious orders, also wear clothes which symbolize their way of life and commitment to God, as do the members of the **Salvation Army**. Christians who belong to this denomination wear a smart uniform. This symbolizes their belief that the Christian faith requires them to live a disciplined and orderly life.

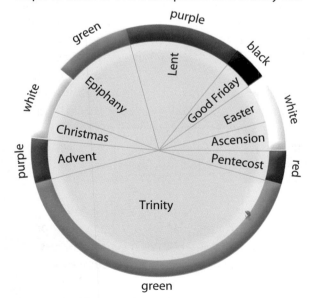

The Christian church has different seasons, represented by various colours

Learning about religion

❶ In groups, research, compare and contrast the Christian use of symbolism with other religious traditions.

❷ Produce a dance routine or mime using symbolic actions which demonstrates a range of feelings Christians might express towards God.

❸ In St John's Gospel there are seven symbols given for Jesus. Look up the following references to find out what they are and produce a 'Symbols for Jesus' poster which could be displayed in church. John 6: 35; 8: 12; 10: 9; 10: 11; 11: 25; 14: 6; 15: 1.

Learning from religion

❶ 'We don't need symbols now we have modern technologies to help us communicate.' Discuss.

❷ Produce four pictures, using colour only, to represent the seasons of the year.

❸ Describe how your life is affected by symbols and explain how you use symbolism in your everyday life.

Worship

In this section you will:

- learn about Christian worship
- discover why Christians worship God
- study the main features of a Christian church
- have the opportunity to write about a place which is special or sacred to you and reflect upon how people should behave in a place of worship.

Worship means paying special attention to something. When **Christians** worship they show that God is important to them. Worshipping God is central to Christianity. Christians worship God for one or more of the following reasons:

- to show their love for God
- to demonstrate their commitment to God
- to thank or praise God
- to ask God for help or guidance in their daily lives
- to ask God for forgiveness
- to strengthen their faith and become closer to God.

Where do Christians worship?

Christians can worship together in public or on their own in private. The main day on which Christians gather together to worship God is on a Sunday. Sunday is the Christian **holy** day. The word 'holy' means 'to do with God'. One reason why Christians have set Sunday aside as a special day of rest and worship is because this is the day on which they believe Jesus rose from the dead. Christians worship God in a variety of buildings such as a private home, abbey, chapel, cathedral, minster, citadel and **church**.

The majority of Christians worship God in a church. There are thousands of Christian churches throughout the world. In Christianity, the word 'church' has several meanings. 'Church' with a capital 'C' refers to different **denominations** or the worldwide Christian community. The word 'church' with a small 'c' refers to the building in which many Christians worship.

A church is regarded as a sacred place. Christians treat their place of worship and the objects in it with great respect.

Features of a Christian place of worship

Traditionally, churches were designed in the shape of a **cross**, the main symbol of Christianity. They were built facing east in the direction of the rising sun. The rising sun marks the beginning of a new day. It is a source of light and life and symbolizes the Christian belief in

Pulpit - a raised platform from where the clergy give a **sermon** to the **congregation**.

Vestry – a room where the official clothing of the clergy are kept, along with robes that the choir wear.

Nave – this is where the congregation sit. They sit on seats called **pews**.

Font – The font is a large stone container which holds holy water. It is where people, usually infants, are baptized.

Chancel – the front area of the church.

Choir stalls

Altar or Holy Table – a raised table where the **Eucharist** or Holy Communion takes place.

Lectern – a stand on which the Bible is placed when it is read out loud.

Side chapel – a small section of the church which has its own altar. It is used for private prayer or special services.

Pews

The main features of an Anglican church

Jesus' **resurrection**. East is also the direction of Jerusalem, the place where Christians believe Jesus died and rose from the dead. Modern churches have been built in many different shapes and sizes and in a variety of locations. Christians have also adapted other buildings and made them into churches.

Modern churches sometimes have the altar in the centre of the church. This reflects the involvement of the laity, ordinary members of the congregation.

Roman Catholic churches usually have the same features as traditional Anglican churches but they also have some additional characteristics.

Learning about religion

❶ Imagine you are a Christian. Write a letter to a friend explaining why worship is important to you.

❷ Design a modern place of worship for Christians and explain the significance of the key features.

❸ Explain what a Christian place of worship can tell us about Christian beliefs. Provide examples to support your statements

Learning from religion

❶ Describe a place which is special or sacred to you and explain why it is important.

❷ Imagine that you are in charge of a school visit to a place of worship. Write a code of conduct for pupils to follow. Explain the reasons for your rules.

❸ 'Churches are a waste of space. You can worship God anywhere.' Find out whether the members of your class agree or disagree with this statement and why.

Ways of worshipping

In this section you will:

● learn about how Christians worship God

● find out about the different ways Christians worship and look at some of the things they use to help them

● have the opportunity to reflect upon some of the issues raised such as the value of silence and how to improve your concentration.

How do Christians worship?

There are two different styles of **Christian** worship. Some Christians prefer to worship God in a formal or structured way. This is called liturgical worship. Liturgical worship involves following a set pattern of rituals called a **liturgy**. This kind of worship is colourful, dramatic and full of symbolism. Worshippers express many of their beliefs by using symbolic objects and performing symbolic actions. Most Churches have their liturgies written down in a book which worshippers follow during services.

Other Christians choose to worship God in a less formal and unstructured way. They have fewer rituals and use less symbolism. This is called non-liturgical worship. In non-liturgical worship the emphasis is on the written or spoken word. Hymns, prayers, Bible readings, **sermons** and personal testimonies are important. This form of worship is found in **Protestant** churches. The Anglican Church, however, uses liturgical worship.

Many Christians believe that worship should not just be confined to church. They think that their everyday lives should be an act of worship. This means praising and being thankful to God in everything they do. Christians say that even the most ordinary things they do take on new meaning when they remember God.

The Eucharist

The most important set service or liturgy is the **Eucharist**. During this service Christians remember the final meal Jesus had with his disciples now called the **Last Supper**. They share a symbolic meal of bread and wine together and reflect upon Jesus' death. The bread symbolizes his body and the wine represents his blood. Different **denominations** call the Eucharist by different names and celebrate it in various ways. They also have different beliefs about what happens to the bread and wine during the ceremony. Many Christians believe that it actually becomes the body and blood of Jesus and he is therefore really present during the service. This idea is known as **transubstantiation**.

The Eucharist is a **sacrament**. A sacrament is an event or experience where Christians believe they receive special blessings from God. Seven activities are regarded as sacraments: **baptism**, Eucharist (also known as **Holy Communion**), **confirmation**, **marriage**, **confession**, **ordination** and **Anointing of the Sick**. Sacraments are particularly important to Roman Catholics.

Aids to worship

Different denominations use different things to help them worship. This table shows the variety of things Christians might use during worship.

Incense
Incense creates atmosphere. It is a sweet smelling gum or spice which gives off odour and smoke when burnt. The incense container or censer is swung from a chain during worship. The smoke rises and this represents prayers which are making their way to God.

Music
A wide range of musical instruments are used during worship. Music is used as an accompaniment to hymns, prayers, **psalms** and other religious songs.

Singing

Worshippers also express their ideas, feelings and beliefs by singing hymns, prayers, psalms and other religious songs. In some Churches there is no musical accompaniment. Orthodox Christians believe that the human voice is the finest thing to use when worshipping God and nothing must detract from this.

Silence

Periods of silence can help the worshipper to concentrate and focus on God.

Candles

A variety of candles are lit during worship. They represent the goodness and light of God which shines in a dark and sinful world.

Cross and crucifix

The **cross** is the symbol of Christianity. It helps Christians to focus and reminds them of Jesus' resurrection. A crucifix is a cross with a figure of Jesus on it.

Bread and wine

Christians share bread and wine together during some services. Jesus asked his disciples to do this in memory of him. The bread represents Jesus' body and the wine his blood.

Icons

An icon is a holy picture representing Jesus, the **Virgin Mary** or another **saint**. They help Christians to focus on God. Worshippers pray and place lit candles in front of icons. They believe that Jesus and saints like the Virgin Mary are already in the presence of God and they hope that they will intercede on their behalf and help them to communicate with God. Icons are mainly used by Orthodox Christians and are objects of great devotion. They are carried in processions during festivals.

Statues

Christians focus on statues of saints like the Virgin Mary, the mother of Jesus, during worship. Worshippers pray and place lit candles in front of statues. They believe that Jesus and saints like the Virgin Mary are already in the presence of God and they hope that they will intercede on their behalf and help them to communicate with God.

Actions

Worshippers express their ideas, feelings and beliefs by performing certain actions such as clapping, dancing, kneeling and genuflecting. They might also put their arms around each other or shake hands as a sign of peace.

The Bible

Passages from the Bible are read during most services.

Service book

A service book sets out the order of service. It tells the worshipper what to do and say.

Rosary

A rosary is a string of beads with a crucifix attached. They are mainly used by Roman Catholics who pass the beads between their thumb and forefinger whilst they are praying.

Learning about religion

❶ 'All Christians should worship the same way.' How do you think a Christian might respond to this statement? Give reasons for your answers.

❷ Research and prepare an information booklet on the seven sacraments of the Christian Church. Explain what they involve and why they are important to Christians.

❸ In groups, produce a game or quiz which teaches younger children about the things Christians use to help them worship.

Learning from religion

❶ Think about someone who is important to you. Write about some things you could do to show them that they are special.

❷ Somebody once said, 'silence is golden' – what do you think they meant by this? Evaluate the importance of stillness and silence in today's busy world.

❸ What advice would you give a friend if they were having trouble concentrating? Make a list of things they could do to help them focus.

Prayer

Christians believe that you can develop a personal relationship with God. One way they do this is through **prayer**. Prayer is a way of communicating with God. It involves talking and listening to God. Many Christians look upon God as their best friend and prayer is a very important part of their everyday life and worship.

How and why do Christians pray?

Christians pray in various ways. They can pray on their own or in a group. Prayers can be said spontaneously on the spur of the moment or at set times. They can be said out loud or silently inside a person's head. Christians can adopt various positions for prayer. Sometimes they kneel down, put their hands together and close their eyes. At other times they might sit or stand.

Christians pray for a variety of reasons. One of the main reasons Christians pray is to improve their relationship with God. They also pray because they believe that prayer can change things. Christians believe in the 'power of prayer'. The following are examples of why Christians say they pray.

Christians are taught to love and pray for their enemies (Matthew 5: 44)

'One of the reasons I pray is:

…because I want God to know that I love him

…to let God know that he is important to me

…to say sorry for the things I have done wrong and ask God to forgive me

…to try and be a better person

… to ask for guidance

…to gain strength if I am having a difficult time

…to ask for help for myself and others

…because I can't help it. Something inside me just makes me want to talk to God

…because Jesus told us to

…to say thank you to God for all the good things in my life

… to find out what God wants me to do.'

What kind of prayers do Christians use?

There are five main forms of prayer which Christians use:

1. Adoration – the person praying focuses on God's greatness and power. They think about how special and important God is.

2. Confession – the person praying focuses on what God expects of them. They think about the things they have done wrong and ask God for forgiveness.

3. Intercession – the person praying focuses on the needs of others. They think about people who need help or guidance and ask God to assist them.

4. Petition – the person praying focuses on their personal needs. They ask God for help and guidance.

5. Thanksgiving – the person praying focuses on God's love and generosity. They think about what God has done for them and say thank you.

Meditation is another form of prayer. It is a quiet form of praying. The person praying is still and silent. They focus on God and try very hard not to think about anything else.

Christians can make up their own prayers or they can use prayers which have been written by other people. One of the most well-known Christian prayers is the Lord's Prayer. This prayer is found in the **Gospels** in Matthew 6: 9–13. Christians believe that Jesus taught this prayer to his disciples. It is used during most acts of Christian worship.

Learning about religion

1. Describe the different forms of prayer a Christian might use and evaluate the role of prayer in their life.

2. Read Luke 11: 5–12. Explain what you think Jesus was saying about prayer.

3. 'Instead of praying about something you should just get on and sort it out yourself.' How do you think Christians would respond to this statement? Give reasons for your answer.

Learning from religion

1. Think about someone who is important to you. Explain what you could do to improve your relationship with them.

2. Make a list of the people you talk and listen to every day and note what kinds of conversations you have. Categorize them according to what they are about. Compare your findings with others in your class. What do you all talk about the most?

3. In some places of Christian worship, visitors can write a prayer request on a piece of paper. The congregation will then pray on your behalf. Write out your own prayer request: state who or what you would like a prayer said for and explain why.

Festivals

In this section you will:

- learn about the main Christian festivals
- find out when they occur and what they commemorate
- have the opportunity to reflect upon some of the issues raised such as the purpose of festivals and how Christian festivals might affect the lives of non-religious people.

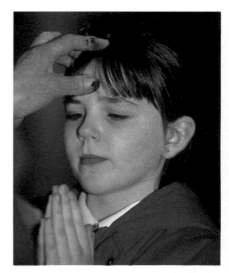

A cross of ash is made on a young worshipper's forehead

Festivals usually celebrate or commemorate a significant event. Most festivals remember an event in the past but they can also look to the future like the Chinese New Year. Festivals can be religious or **secular** occasions.

The main **Christian** festivals are based on significant events in Jesus' life. The date of Christian festivals can change, only Christmas and Epiphany fall on the same date each year. This is because festival dates are determined by the date of **Easter Day** which is always the Sunday after the full moon in March. The exact date of Easter can vary by several weeks.

Epiphany – 6 January

Epiphany remembers how the Magi or Wise Men from the East came to visit the newborn baby Jesus. The Magi were the first Gentiles (non-Jews) to visit Jesus. This festival celebrates them recognizing his special status. Epiphany marks the end of the Christmas period. Traditionally, it is the day when all the Christmas decorations should be taken down and put away.

Ash Wednesday – February/March

Ash Wednesday is a day of humility and penitence. It is a time when Christians show they

are sorry for the things they have done wrong. One way some of them do this is by going to a special church service where the **priest** smears a cross of ash on their foreheads. The ash comes from the burning of the previous year's palm crosses, crosses made from palm leaves which are given to worshippers on **Palm Sunday**. Ash Wednesday also marks the beginning of Lent, a time of fasting and prayer in preparation for Easter.

Easter – March/April

Easter is the most important festival in the Christian Church. It begins on **Good Friday** when Christians commemorate the suffering and death of Jesus and ends on Easter Sunday when they celebrate their belief in his **resurrection**.

Ascension Day – May/June

Ascension Day is when Christians celebrate their belief that Jesus left the earth and ascended (went up) into the presence of God 40 days after his resurrection. The state of being with God after death is known as Heaven.

'…He was taken up to Heaven as they watched him…' (Acts 1: 9)

Trinity Sunday – May/June

Trinity Sunday is when Christians celebrate their belief in the Trinity. The Trinity is the Christian idea that there is one God who has made Himself known to the world in three ways: Father, Son and Holy Spirit.

Christmas – 25 December

Christmas is a twelve-day celebration which commemorates the birth of Jesus. No one knows exactly when Jesus was born. About 300 years after Jesus' death, Christians took over a mid-winter **pagan** festival and dedicated it to Jesus' birth.

Pentecost – May/June

At Pentecost Christians celebrate the giving of the **Holy Spirit** to Jesus' followers and the founding of the Christian Church. In the **New Testament** it says that just before Jesus ascended to heaven he promised his disciples that God would send them a helper. This helper was called the Holy Spirit, who would support and guide them. The New Testament also says that ten days later whilst the early Christians were celebrating the Jewish festival of Shavuot (Feast of Weeks), there was a gushing wind and flames of fire and the Holy Spirit came amongst them. This made them realize that they must spread the 'Good News' about Jesus. Christians look upon this event as the official beginning or the birthday of the Christian Church.

In this country, Pentecost is also known as Whitsun or 'White Sunday'. This is because it became a popular day for baptisms and the people entering the Christian Church wore white as a symbol of purity.

Learning about religion

❶ Describe how the various Christian festivals reflect key events in Jesus' life.

❷ Explain what Christian festivals can tell us about Christian beliefs.

❸ Make a card you could send to a Christian on one of their festivals, which recognizes the religious significance of the event.

Learning from religion

❶ Explain what you would have a festival for and why.

❷ 'Festivals are just an excuse to have fun.' Do you agree? Give reasons for your answer.

❸ Explain some of the ways that Christian festivals might affect non-religious people.

Christmas and Easter

In this section you will:

● learn what the festivals of Easter and Christmas mean to Christians and find out how they prepare for and celebrate Christmas

● have the opportunity to reflect upon some of the issues raised such as different ways of giving and the importance of new beginnings.

Easter and Christmas are the two most important festivals in Christianity.

Christmas remembers Jesus' birth and celebrates the **Incarnation**. Christmas is also a time of thanksgiving. **Christians** think that, through Jesus, God gave himself to the world. He became involved in the lives of human beings and changed things for the better.

Easter is the most significant of all Christian festivals. It remembers Jesus' death and celebrates the Christian belief that Jesus rose from the dead. The events of Easter honour Jesus and remind Christians of who he was and what he did for them. Easter also gives Christians hope for the future. It celebrates the Christian belief that there is life after death and that good always triumphs over evil.

Christians understand Jesus' life and death in a particular way. They think that his life and death had a purpose. Christians believe that Jesus made it possible for human beings to have a close personal relationship with God. They say that before Jesus was born human beings had forgotten about God and the way He or She wanted them to live. People lived according to their own selfish desires and committed many sins. Christians say that Jesus changed things.

He reminded people about God and taught them the right way to live. Jesus also put right the wrongs of the past. Christians believe that

Jesus' death made up or atoned for the sins of human beings and reconciled or brought together human beings and God. This is why the day Jesus died is called **Good Friday** because something very good happened as a result of his death.

The **resurrection** has several meanings for Christians. Most importantly, they believe it proves that Jesus was the Son of God and that he is alive today. It is also seen as a sign of God's **forgiveness** and proof that life continues after death.

Jesus is often called **Redeemer** because he redeemed or 'brought back' people to God. Jesus is also referred to as a **Saviour** because he saved people from the consequences of their sin and death. **Atonement**, **Redemption**, **Reconciliation**, **Salvation** and **Eternal Life** are important ideas in Christianity.

How do Christians celebrate Christmas?

The four weeks before Christmas are known as Advent. The word 'advent' means 'coming'. Advent is a period of preparation before Christmas. During Advent, Christians think about Jesus coming to the world as a baby and what this meant for human beings. Christians believe that Jesus was the **Messiah**, a saviour sent by God to bring goodness and peace to the Earth.

Counting the days until Christmas

Christians enjoy celebrating Christmas, but they also think carefully about the meaning of the festival

Christians also read and reflect upon passages from the Bible which talk about the Messiah and what He will be like. Another thing Christians think about is the future, as they believe Jesus promised his disciples that he would return to Earth one day to judge people and to decide who should go to Heaven. This is known as the **Second Coming** as it will be the second time Jesus has been to Earth.

Carols are a sung throughout the Christmas period. A carol is a hymn about Jesus' birth. Some Christians light Advent candles and use Advent calendars to count the days to Christmas Day. Houses and many churches are also decorated with Christmas trees and coloured lights. Light is used a lot at Christmas. This represents the Christian belief that Jesus is the light of the world. Christmas is sometimes called a festival of light because it celebrates the birth of Jesus whom Christians call 'light of the world'. Christians also believe that Jesus was God's gift to the world. This is where the idea of people giving and receiving presents comes from.

Most Christians try to go to church at Christmas and take part in the **Eucharist**. One of the most popular services at Christmas is called the **Midnight Mass** which begins at about 11.30pm on Christmas Eve.

What do Christians say about Christmas?

'…Many people have forgotten the real meaning of Christmas … it's not about tinsel, selection boxes and presents … it's about Jesus!'

'…I especially try to follow Jesus' example at Christmas … I think about people who are less fortunate than myself and try to help them.'

'…I love all the lights of Christmas … I think light is a good way to represent Jesus because his goodness shines and stands out against the darkness of evil.'

Learning about religion

❶ Draw a diagram which shows and explains how the Christian ideas of Atonement, Redemption, Reconciliation, Salvation and Eternal Life are connected to each other.

❷ In pairs role-play, in turn, a Christian and a non-Christian. Explain to each other what the festivals of Christmas and Easter mean from a religious and non-religious viewpoint.

❸ Write an Easter hymn or Christmas carol which Christians might sing during these festivals.

Learning from religion

❶ Have you ever fallen out with someone and made it up again? Describe what happened.

❷ Make a list of reasons why people might need a new beginning or to start again in some way.

❸ Discuss in groups what you can give to people apart from material things.

Easter

In this section you will:

● find out how Christians prepare for and celebrate Easter

● look at what some Christians say about Easter

● have the opportunity to reflect upon some of the issues raised such as the idea of giving up things for an important reason.

A Palm Sunday procession

How do Christians celebrate Easter?

Traditionally, **Christians** begin preparing for Easter on Shrove Tuesday, the day before Ash Wednesday, the beginning of Lent. Shrove Tuesday is also known as 'Pancake Day'. It is called 'Pancake Day' because in the past Christians followed a very strict diet during Lent and didn't eat any rich foods. Foods such as eggs, milk and flour were considered luxuries so they were used up to make pancakes before the Lenten fast began. Today, most Christians try to give up something they usually enjoy eating for Lent, such as chocolate.

Lent lasts for 40 days and ends on Easter Sunday. It lasts for this amount of time because Christianity teaches that Jesus spent 40 days and nights in the desert being tempted by the Devil before he began his ministry. Lent is a solemn and serious time for the Christian **Church**. Some Churches have traditions which symbolize this like flowers being taken out of the church and the covering up of icons and other religious objects.

The last week of Lent is known as **Holy Week**. This is when Christians remember the final seven days of Jesus' life. It begins with **Palm Sunday** and includes **Maundy Thursday**, **Good Friday** and **Holy Saturday**.

According to the **New Testament**, Jesus came to Jerusalem to celebrate the Jewish festival of **Pesach** (Passover). He rode on a donkey and was welcomed by people waving palm leaves and placing them in his path. Palm Sunday is when Christians commemorate Jesus' entry into Jerusalem. Many churches hand out **crosses** made of palm leaves in memory of this event.

Maundy Thursday is when Christians remember the final meal or **Last Supper** Jesus had with his disciples and his arrest in the Garden of Gethsemane. In some Christian communities the **priest** will wash the feet of his or her congregation. This reminds worshippers of the sacrifice Jesus made and demonstrates the Christian belief that everyone is equal in the eyes of God.

Russian Orthodox Christians kiss the coffin of Christ on Good Friday

Good Friday is when Christians mourn the death of Jesus. It the saddest day in the Christian year. Churches are stripped of their usual decorations and the colour of soft furnishings, like the altar frontals, are changed to black. Many Christians spend between 12.00pm and 3.00pm, the time Jesus is believed to have spent on the cross, in church meditating on the suffering and death of Jesus. Some Christians also take part in processions and the Orthodox Church holds a kind of funeral for Jesus.

Holy Saturday is the last day of Lent. During the day, churches are cleaned and decorated with flowers, in preparation for **Easter Day**. Christians attend a late evening service called the Easter Vigil. The word 'vigil' means 'to keep watch' and worshippers wait expectantly for Easter Day to arrive. The service starts in darkness, with the exception of a few candles so that the Bible can be read. Gradually, the church becomes filled with light as worshippers light candles from the **paschal candle**. The paschal candle represents the light of Jesus; and the change from darkness to light represents the Christian belief that Jesus overcame death and good triumphed over evil.

Easter Sunday is when Christians celebrate their belief that Jesus came back to life after he died. This is known as the resurrection and there are many traditions and customs associated with this important Christian event. It is a very joyful occasion and Christians make a special effort to go to church and take part in the **Eucharist**. Some Churches begin the day with a bonfire at dawn. They also hard boil eggs and paint them. The eggs are symbols of new life. Chocolate Easter eggs, which many people enjoy eating, have developed from this idea.

What do Christians say about Easter?

'…On Good Friday I mourn Jesus. I feel His pain and suffering. On Easter Sunday I feel happy. I know that Jesus is alive and I celebrate His victory over death.'

'…Easter reminds me that there is life after death … I think about people I have known who have died … and I feel happy to think that I will see them again one day.'

'…Easter is a time of new beginnings … Jesus sacrificed himself so that we could have a fresh start with God.'

'Easter reminds me that with God everything is possible … the Holy Spirit brought Jesus back to life … imagine what it can do for ordinary people!'

Learning about religion

❶ Imagine you are a Christian. Write a diary account of Holy Week explaining what these events mean to you.

❷ Read John 20: 1–18 in the New Testament and describe what Christians believe happened on the first Easter morning.

❸ Design a poster showing the symbols associated with Easter and explain what they can tell us about Christian beliefs.

Learning from religion

❶ If you had to give up something for six weeks, to demonstrate your commitment to something, what would you give up and why?

❷ Conduct a class survey to find out which day of the year is most important to members of your class and why.

❸ 'Only Christians should eat Easter eggs.' Do you agree? Give reasons for your answers.

Pilgrimage 1

In this section you will:

● learn about Christian pilgrimage

● find out why Christians might go on a pilgrimage and look at some of the sites they could visit

● have the chance to explain where you would most like to visit and reflect on the reasons why people might seek peace and quiet.

A **pilgrimage** is a religious journey. It is also a form of worship. A person who goes on a pilgrimage is called a **pilgrim**. Pilgrims visit places they believe to be holy or sacred. A place is usually considered holy or sacred if something of religious importance has happened there, such as a miraculous event or the birth of a leader or teacher. Sites of pilgrimage can be found in a variety of locations. People can make pilgrimages on their own or go with others.

People go on pilgrimages for different reasons:

- to strengthen their faith and become closer to God

- to show commitment to their religion

- to say thank you for something good which has happened

- to make up for something they have done wrong (**penance**)

- to ask for help or healing

- to fulfil their religious duty

- to follow tradition or to satisfy their curiosity.

Most people think of pilgrimage as an actual physical journey to a particular place. It can also refer to our journey through life from birth to death. Another understanding of pilgrimage is that it can refer to an inner journey. An inner journey is the process by which we learn more about ourselves as we grow and develop.

One of the ways **Christians** find out more about themselves, and what they believe God wants of them, is by going on a retreat. When Christians go on retreat they take a break from their normal lives. They stay in a quiet and peaceful place and spend time thinking and praying.

Where do Christians go on pilgrimage?

There are many Christian holy sites all over the world. Most are 'official' sites of pilgrimage. This means that the Christian Church has accepted that something special has happened there. There are also 'unofficial' sites of pilgrimage where people claim extraordinary and supernatural things have taken place but they are not officially recognized by the Church.

The Holy Land

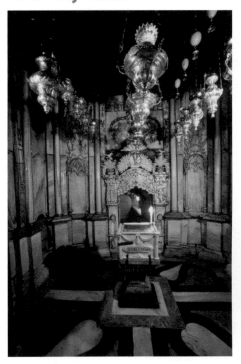

The tomb of Christ in the Church of the Holy Sepulchre, Jerusalem, is an important pilgrimage site for Christians

Israel is the country where Jesus lived. It is also known as the Holy Land because it contains many holy sites. Israel is a very popular place of pilgrimage. Pilgrims like to (literally) follow in the footsteps of Jesus and visit the places associated with him. These include Bethlehem, the town where he was born, Nazareth where Jesus grew up and Jerusalem, the place of his crucifixion and **resurrection**.

Rome

Rome in Italy is an important pilgrimage site for Christians as it was a centre for the early Church. Many of the early Christians, including the **apostles** Peter and Paul, were martyred there. Pilgrims can visit the Catacombs, underground burial chambers where the early Christians used to meet and worship in secret. Pilgrims can also see the Vatican and St Peter's Basilica. The Vatican is the home of the Pope, the leader of the Roman Catholic Church. St Peter's Basilica is very a beautiful church dedicated to Peter who was the first Pope. The church was built on the site of Peter's grave and there is a **shrine** inside dedicated to him.

Lourdes

Millions of pilgrims visit Lourdes every year to pray and receive healing

Another famous place of pilgrimage is Lourdes in France. Lourdes is where a fourteen-year-old French girl called Bernadette Soubirous is believed to have seen the **Virgin Mary**, Jesus' mother, in 1858. The **apparition** appeared in a grotto near the banks of a river. She emphasized the importance of **prayer** and **penance** and requested that a chapel be built. The Virgin Mary also told Bernadette to dig in the mud. A spring appeared which is believed to have healing properties. Many people claim to have been miraculously cured from serious illnesses or disabilities after bathing in the spring.

Learning about religion

1. Explain how a Christian might benefit by going on a pilgrimage. Use examples of sites to support your statements.

2. Write a prayer which a Christian might say at a place of pilgrimage.

3. Design a poster advertising a Christian retreat.

Learning from religion

1. Explain where you would most like to visit and why.

2. Draw a symbolic road which represents your journey through life. Use one symbol a year to represent a key event which happened during that time. Explain what each symbol represents and why you have chosen it. Remember the shape of your road can also be symbolic.

3. Make a list of the reasons why people might seek quiet and peaceful places to think about things.

> In this section you will:
> - look at some sites of Christian pilgrimage
> - have the opportunity to discuss some of the issues raised such as the authenticity of visions and whether you should keep secrets from people.

Fatima

Fatima, in Portugal, is a very popular Roman Catholic **pilgrimage** site. Fatima is where three children, Lucia de Jesus, aged ten, and her cousins Francisco and Jacinta Marto, aged nine and seven, are believed to have seen the **Virgin Mary** in 1917. The **apparition**, who was described as a 'Lady more brilliant than the sun', emphasized the importance of **prayer** and **penance**. She also told Lucia three secrets called the Secrets of Fatima. The first secret was a vision of hell, believed to refer to the two world wars. The second secret was a vision of peace.

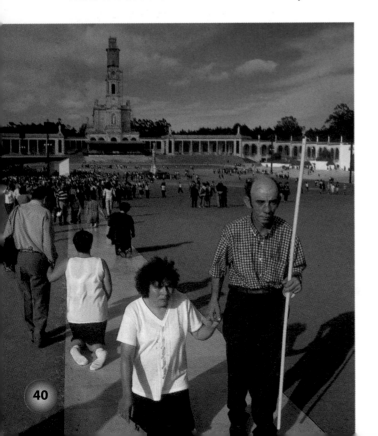

Only part of the third secret has been revealed. The Vatican, the centre of authority for the Roman Catholic Church, says that it involves martyrdom and suffering. It has been linked with the failed assassination attempt on Pope John Paul II in 1981.

Pilgrims visiting Fatima sometimes approach the shrine on their knees as a penance. This shows that they are sorry for the things they have done wrong. They also buy and light large candles, which they place in a big furnace. The candles are usually lit for someone or something and a prayer is said as they are put into the fire.

Walsingham

Some people regard Walsingham in Norfolk as an **ecumenical** pilgrimage site. This is because **Christians** from different **denominations** go there on pilgrimage. Walsingham is where Richeldis de Faverches is believed to have had a vision of the Virgin Mary in 1061. The apparition showed her Jesus' home in Nazareth and Richeldis built a replica of the house she had seen. When Christians visit the Holy House they think about Jesus' childhood and adolescence. It also reminds them of the **Incarnation**. The Holy House represents the important Christian belief that Jesus was the Son of God but he also had a human mother and family.

Medjugorje

Medjugorje in Bosnia is a modern unofficial pilgrimage site. Since 1981, six young people who live in this village claim to have seen more than 300 visions of the Virgin Mary. The visionaries say that the Virgin Mary's purpose for coming to Earth is to guide people back to God. She is also believed to have left behind proof of her visitations in the form of miraculously appearing images. Many Christians visit Medjugorje in the hope of finding peace. The word 'Medjugorje' means 'between the hills'. It has been described as a 'place where Heaven touches the Earth'.

Many retreats are held in Christian settings such as a monastery or abbey

Iona

Iona is a small island off the west coast of Scotland. It is a place of pilgrimage and retreat. Iona was originally the home of St Columba, an Irish Christian prince. He established a monastery there when he was forced to leave Ireland in 563 CE. Today, Iona is an ecumenical Christian community with 240 members from a variety of backgrounds and denominations. Iona is a symbol of Christian unity. It shows that different Christian groups can live, work and worship together.

Members of the community don't have to spend all of their time on Iona but they do need to follow the 'rules' of the community wherever they are. They must:

● take part in regular acts of worship (which includes praying for half an hour each morning)

● be prepared to share what they have with others

● account for the way they use their time and money

● meet with other members of the community (three times on the mainland and for a week in the summer on Iona)

● work for justice and peace.

Ordinary Christians can spend time on Iona either as volunteers, employees or pilgrims on retreat. The community also runs a youth organization and young people can stay on the island during their holidays. Most people who have visited Iona agree that it is a beautiful and special place. They come back home feeling rested and closer to God.

Learning about religion

❶ Imagine that you work for a travel company which specializes in arranging tours for pilgrims. Research a pilgrimage site and prepare a brochure which tells Christians about the place and encourages them to visit as pilgrims.

❷ Discuss in groups what else you think the third secret of Fatima might say and suggest reasons why it has been kept a secret.

❸ Imagine that the Pope has asked you, on behalf of the Roman Catholic Church, to investigate what has been happening at Medjugorje. Make up some tests you could carry out to decide whether the visions were genuine.

Learning from religion

❶ 'People don't really have visions. They just make up these stories to get attention.' Do you agree with this statement? Explain your reasons.

❷ Provide an illustration to match the phrase 'a place where Heaven touches the Earth.'

❸ Discuss in groups whether you should keep secrets from people.

Baptism

Believers' baptisms are happy and joyous occasions

In this section you will:

- learn about the Christian rites of passage
- find out why baptism is important to Christians and what happens during an infant baptism
- have the opportunity to discuss what stages in life you would like to celebrate
- be able to reflect upon some of the issues raised such as the responsibilities people have towards children in their care.

Many **Christians** look upon life as a pilgrimage. They say that life is a journey from the 'cradle to the grave'. Christians believe that they are given life by God at the beginning of their time on Earth and return to God at the end. **Rites of passage** are special ceremonies which mark important events along the way. They are called rites of passage because the ceremonies have rituals (or rites) which are associated with the passing of time on Earth.

The four main Christian rites of passage are **baptism**, **confirmation**, **marriage** and **death**. Baptism, confirmation and marriage and are also known as **sacraments** by many Christians. A sacrament is an event or experience where Christians believe they receive special blessings from God.

Baptism

Christians think that **baptism** is important because it is the ceremony by which people enter the Christian faith and become members of the Christian **Church**. The **Gospels** say that Jesus was baptized in the River Jordan by his cousin, John the Baptist. They also say that Jesus asked his followers to be baptized.

Christians believe that by being baptized they are following Jesus' example and doing what he asked. Jesus' baptism marks the beginning of his public ministry. When Christians are baptized it marks the beginning of their life as a Christian.

What happens during baptism?

Some **denominations** baptize people when they are babies. This is known as **infant baptism**. Another name for baptism is christening. The word 'christening' comes from the idea of being given a name in Christ (as a Christian). This is because part of the baptism ceremony involves being given a Christian name.

Baptism takes place in a church. It can be part of an ordinary service or a private ceremony. Traditionally, the baby is dressed in white as a symbol of purity and goodness.

Parents and godparents gather round the font and take vows on the baby's behalf and promise to help bring them up in the Christian faith. The parents name the child and the vicar or **priest** makes the sign of the **cross** on the baby's forehead. **Holy water** is poured from the font onto the baby's head three times, once for each member of the **Trinity**: Father, Son and **Holy Spirit**.

This method of baptism is known as affusion. Water is a very important symbol during baptism. This is because Christianity teaches that everyone is born in a state of **sin**. This belief is called the doctrine of original sin. The doctrine of original sin is based on the idea that the very first human beings disobeyed God and their sins have been passed on to every human being since. When water is poured on the baby it represents spiritual cleansing, the idea of washing away sins and starting again. This means that the baby can no longer be blamed for things human beings have done wrong before it was born. In Roman Catholic baptisms the baby is also anointed with oil on the chest and head. During Orthodox baptisms the baby (or adult) is completely immersed in water three times which symbolizes a belief in the Trinity, the death of past sins and a new life in Jesus. This method of baptism is known as immersion.

At the end of the ceremony, some Churches hand a small lighted candle to the baby's parents. This signifies that the baby now belongs to Jesus, the light of the world.

Other denominations like the Baptist and Pentecostal Churches do not believe in baptizing babies. Babies are usually welcomed into the church with a special service of Infant Dedication. Baptism is delayed until the child grows up and requests it. This is known as a **believer's baptism**. It is seen as a very powerful act of personal witness to their faith in Jesus. Personal witness is when someone provides evidence of their faith. Churches which practise believer's baptism think that you must make a personal choice to follow Jesus when you are old enough to understand what the commitment involves. This often happens when people are teenagers, but the age of believers' baptisms can vary. During the service, they publicly take vows and commit themselves to the Christian faith. Believers are also symbolically immersed in water which illustrates their belief in spiritual cleansing, the idea of washing away sin.

Believers' baptisms are usually held in a church building which contains a **baptistry**. A baptistry is a small pool which contains enough water for believers to be fully immersed. Believers' baptism can also take place in the sea or in a river or swimming pool. The River Jordan in Israel, where Jesus is believed to have been baptized, is a popular place for believers' baptisms.

Learning about religion

❶ Imagine that you are a Christian parent trying to arrange a baptism for your baby. Write to a friend inviting them to the ceremony and explain why you have decided to have your child baptized.

❷ Explain why you think many churches now prefer to baptize babies in their normal services instead of having a private ceremony.

❸ Describe some of the ways a Christian upbringing might be different to a non-Christian upbringing.

Learning from religion

❶ What rites of passage or stages in life would you like to celebrate and why?

❷ In the Church of England, godparents have five main responsibilities towards their godchildren. What do you think are the main responsibilities a person has towards a child in their care?

❸ 'People should wait until they are eighteen before they commit to a religion.' Do you agree? Give reasons for your answer, supporting your statements.

Confirmation

In this section you will:

● learn about a Christian rite of passage called confirmation

● find out why confirmation is important to Christians and what happens during a confirmation service

● have the opportunity to reflect on some of the issues raised such as making your own decisions and discuss the things which make you feel grown up and important.

Confirmation is important to some **Christians** because it is the service by which they become full adult members of the Christian Church. Confirmation is when they publicly confirm the vows made on their behalf during **infant** **baptism** and make their own commitment to the Christian way of life. Many Christians believe that confirmation brings them closer to God and improves their relationship with the Church. They also think it enables people to receive strength and guidance from the Holy Spirit. For some Christians, confirmation means that they can accept Holy Communion (bread and wine) during the Eucharist.

What happens during confirmation?

There is no set age for confirmation. Roman Catholics are usually confirmed when they are about eight years old. Traditionally, in the Church of England, adolescence has been a popular time for confirmation. People preparing for confirmation normally attend confirmation

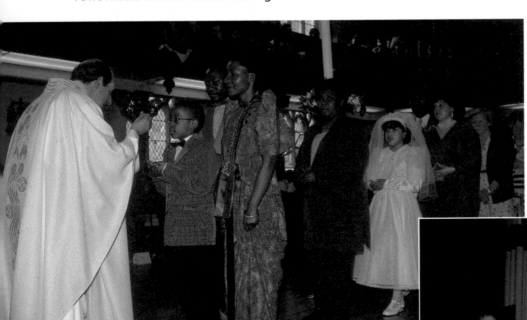

Young Roman Catholics taking their first Holy Communion

The laying on of hands during confirmation is a symbol of blessing

classes run by their local church. This helps them to understand the teachings of the Christian Church and what is expected of them.

Confirmation services are usually conducted by a bishop. During the ceremony, the person being confirmed is asked a series of questions about their beliefs such as, 'Do you believe and trust in God?' Another important feature of the service is when the bishop places his hands on the head of the candidate and prays. The bishop prays that the **Holy Spirit** will strengthen and guide the person being confirmed. In some Churches, the bishop will also put oil on the candidate's forehead. This symbolizes the gifts or blessings that the Holy Spirit will bring.

In Orthodox Churches there is no separate service of confirmation. Confirmation is carried out by a priest straight after baptism. This service is called **chrismation**. Chrismation involves the baby being anointed or smeared with oil on the forehead, eyes, lips, mouth, nostrils, chest, hands and feet. This symbolizes that the Holy Spirit must energize the whole person in **Christ**. The baby is also given their first **Holy Communion** (bread and wine) on the same occasion.

Denominations which perform **believers' baptism** do not have a confirmation ceremony. Like confirmation, the baptism service is the rite by which they become full adult or grown up members of the Christian Church. It enables them to participate fully in religious practices of their denomination.

What do Christians say about confirmation?

'I decided to get confirmed when I was thirteen. It was the first really big decision that I had made about my life. I got confirmed because I wanted to make a personal commitment to the faith into which I was born. I wanted God to know that I was choosing to be a Christian and not just following the tradition of my parents.'

'I enjoyed going to church but I always felt that something was missing because I could never take bread and wine during the Eucharist. After I got confirmed, I really felt part of the community'.

'My confirmation ceremony was a very moving experience. When the bishop put his hands on my head I felt honoured and humble. I prayed that I would be a good Christian.'

Learning about religion

❶ Imagine that you are a young Christian about to be confirmed. Write a dialogue of a telephone conversation between you and a friend in which you invite the ceremony. Explain to them your decision to get confirmed.

❷ Design a card which you could send to a Christian for their confirmation.

❸ Explain what difference confirmation or a believers' baptism might make to a person's life.

Learning from religion

❶ Have you ever been to an important ceremony or had to make a big decision about something? Describe what happened.

❷ At what age are you old enough to make your own decisions? Give reasons for your answer.

❸ Discuss in pairs what kind of things make you feel grown up and important.

Marriage and funerals

In this section you will:

● learn why marriage is important to Christians

● find out what happens during a Christian marriage ceremony and Christian funeral ceremony

● have the opportunity to reflect upon the commitment marriage involves and express your views on the idea of life after death.

Marriage

Christians believe that **marriage** is important because it is a gift or blessing from God. They say that in marriage God brings two people together to love, help and support each other throughout life. The love the couple have for each other is said to reflect the love Jesus had for his followers. Christians believe that through marriage they learn more about God's love for human beings. Christians see marriage as the right relationship for having sexual intercourse and children.

In preparation for their wedding, many couples attend marriage courses run by their church. This helps them to understand the Christian teaching on marriage and the importance of the commitment they are going to make to each other.

What happens during a Christian marriage ceremony?

Each **denomination** has its own marriage ceremony but some features are common to most services. The ceremony usually begins with a hymn which helps people to focus on God. This is followed by a statement which summarizes the purpose of a Christian marriage.

The couple and their guests are then asked if there is any reason they cannot get married. Once the **priest** is satisfied that there are no objections to the marriage, the couple make promises or vows to each other and exchange rings to symbolize their commitment. This is one of the most important parts of the service. Christians believe that they are making their vows before God. The rings, traditionally perfect circles without a beginning or end, symbolize that the promises they have made cannot be broken. Finally, the couple are pronounced husband and wife and prayers are said for them. At the end of the ceremony the newly married couple sign a register to record that the marriage is legal.

In Orthodox churches, after making their vows and exchanging rings, the couple have crowns or garlands placed upon their heads. This symbolizes that the couple have been blessed by God. They also drink wine from the same cup which represents their new life together. Another feature is that the priest leads the couple in a circular procession around the church. This symbolizes that the marriage will have no end.

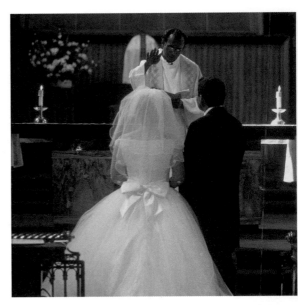

The bride and groom kneel while the priest blesses them

Death

What happens during a Christian funeral?

Christians believe that there is life after death. This idea is called **eternal life**.

A Christian funeral marks the passing of a believer from this life to eternal life. It also gives people the opportunity to express their feelings and beliefs about death and say goodbye to someone they have cared about. Traditionally, mourners wear dark clothing which symbolizes their sadness. Funeral services take place in a church or **crematorium** chapel. The service usually consists of prayers, hymns, readings and a **sermon** about death, **resurrection** and the life of the person who has died. The ceremony reminds Christians that life is a precious gift from God. They also think about Jesus' death and resurrection. Their belief that Jesus came back to life after he had died brings them comfort and gives them hope for the future. It makes them think that they will meet Jesus and be reunited with their loved ones in Heaven one day. After the funeral service, the body is cremated or buried in a consecrated graveyard. This final part of the ceremony is called the committal.

Learning about religion

❶ Write a voiceover script to go with a video of a Christian wedding which explains what happens and why.

❷ Explain how you think Christian beliefs about life after death might affect daily life of Christian.

❸ Imagine that you are a Christian. Write a letter of comfort to someone who has been bereaved which expresses your beliefs about life after death.

Learning from religion

❶ Design your own set of wedding vows which reflect the commitment marriage involves.

❷ Explain what you think happens to us when we die.

❸ Design a storybook to explain the idea of death to a child.

One way Christians remember their loved ones who have died is by dedicating a headstone to them

Creation

In this section you will:

● look at Christian beliefs about Creation

● learn how Christians believe the universe came into existence

● have the opportunity to reflect upon the natural world and write your own creation story.

Day two: God made the sky. He used the sky to divide the water that covered the Earth into two halves.

What do Christians believe about Creation?

Christians believe that God created the universe out of nothing. They say that the wonders and beauty of nature, the complicated way life on earth is arranged and the workings of the solar system means that creation could not have happened by accident. The creation story in Genesis, the first book of the **Old Testament** in the Christian Bible, explains what many Christians believe happened.

Day three: God made land appear from beneath the water. He called the land 'earth' and the water the 'sea'. God also made plants, trees and vegetation to grow on the earth.

The Creation story

When God first created the Universe, the Earth was dark and covered in water.

Day one: God made light and separated it from the darkness. He called the light 'day' and the darkness 'night'.

Day four: God made the sun, moon and stars to light up the sky and separate night from day.

Day five: God made all the creatures that live on the earth. He made fish for the sea, birds for the air and animals and insects for the land.

Day six: God made human beings. He put them in charge of everything he had created and told them to look after it.

Day seven: God rested. The universe was complete.

What is the Christian attitude towards the Creation story?

Christians have different attitudes towards the Creation story. Some fundamentalist Christians believe that the Creation story is an accurate account of what literally happened. Most Christians, however, think that the Creation story is a myth. Myths are stories that explain mysterious events, unusual traditions or extraordinary sights in nature. They are usually ancient and have been passed on by word of mouth for hundreds of years before being written down. Many people think myths contain some truth without being accurate historical accounts or scientific explanations of what they describe.

Some scientists have criticized Christian beliefs about creation. They and others believe in the theory of **evolution**. They say that science has proved that it took much longer than six days for the universe to be formed. Many Christians agree with this. They believe that the word 'day', in the Creation story, is a metaphor for a much longer period of time.

Astronomers have also criticized Christian ideas about creation. They believe that a massive explosion in space about eighteen billion years ago was responsible for the formation of the universe. This is called the Big Bang theory. Christians say that this theory supports their belief that God created the universe out of nothing.

Learning about religion

❶ Outline the Christian Creation story and explain how and why it has been criticized.

❷ Prepare a visual presentation to support the Christian viewpoint that Creation could not have happened by accident.

❸ Discuss in pairs the difficulties a Christian might face because of their beliefs if they were either a scientist or astronomer investigating the origins of the universe.

Learning from religion

❶ Write your own Creation story to explain how the world came into existence.

❷ Describe the most amazing or beautiful thing in nature that you have ever seen.

The environment

In this section you will:

● find out why Christians believe they should look after the environment and learn about some of the ways they care for it

● have the opportunity to identify some of the environmental problems that concern people today

● be able to reflect upon some of the issues raised such as the responsibilities involved in looking after something for someone else.

Why do Christians believe they should care for the environment?

Christians believe that the Earth and everything in it belongs to God. They believe that God appointed human beings to be stewards or managers of the Earth and look after it. The idea that human beings have a responsibility to look after the Earth is known as **stewardship**. Christians also believe that human beings will eventually have to account to God for the way in which they have treated Creation.

Another reason Christians look after the environment is that they realize that they are dependent upon it for things that they need to live such as food, water and oxygen. They are reminded of their dependence upon Creation during weekly worship and at other times during the year. In the autumn Christians have a Harvest Festival. Traditionally, this is a time of celebration, thanksgiving and praise for 'the harvest of the fields' such as fruits, vegetables and grains. Nowadays displays of various foods are made in church and services are held to praise God and thank Him for His goodness.

The food is usually distributed afterwards to the elderly and those in need.

How do Christians care for the environment?

Christians fulfil their responsibility to look after the Earth in a variety of ways. Some of the things they might do include disposing of litter properly, recycling rubbish and only buying products which are packaged using biodegradable materials. They have also set up several Christian organizations which work to protect the environment on a larger scale.

The Christian Ecology Link (CEL) encourages Christians throughout Britain to think seriously about environmental issues. It helps them to understand their responsibilities towards the environment and suggests ways that they can help to protect it. The CEL publishes a magazine called *Green Christians* which informs people about their work. It also organizes events such as a National Car-free Day, a Festival of Cycling and Walk to School Weeks which are designed to focus the public's attention on the damage cars can do to people's health and the environment.

Another organization, the European Christian Environmental Network (ECEN), encourages Christians in 26 countries throughout Europe to get involved in a wide range of environmental work. Some of the issues they deal with include climate change and genetic engineering.

Eurpoean Christian Environmental Network (ECEN) symbol

Christian Ecology Link (CEL) symbol

Christian aid agencies try to set up self-sustainable programmes of development. Here, CAFOD are distributing buckets in Albania

Christian Aid agencies such as CAFOD, Christian Aid and Tearfund have a role to play too. They show how environmental abuse can affect the quality of people's lives. These organizations work in some of the poorest countries of the world and campaign for a more caring and just distribution of the Earth's resources.

Learning about religion

❶ Prepare a report which a Christian could present to God about some of the environmental problems facing the Earth today and the action they are taking to resolve them.

❷ Find out more about one of the Christian organizations mentioned in this section and produce an information leaflet about their work.

❸ Imagine that you are in charge of presenting a 'Good Steward of the Earth' award to a Christian. What criteria would they need to meet and why? Design an application form which would tell you what you needed to know.

Learning from religion

❶ Conduct a class survey to find out which environmental issue concerns people the most. Present your findings in the form of a graph and plan a campaign of action to tackle one of the issues mentioned.

❷ Discuss what else people need to have a good quality of life apart from food, water and oxygen.

❸ Explain which you think brings the greatest responsibility – looking after something for someone else or taking care of your own property. Give reasons for your answer.

Moral issues 1

In this section you will:

- learn how Christians decide what is right and wrong
- find out about the Christian attitude to animal rights
- have the opportunity to express your own views on the issue of animal rights.

What is a moral issue?

Morality is about right and wrong behaviour. A **moral** issue is a situation which might be considered to be right or wrong for a variety of reasons, such as the laws of a country, the teachings of a religion or the beliefs and values of an individual or community. A moral decision is where a choice has to be made between what is the right thing to do and the wrong thing to do. Not all the decisions people have to make are moral decisions.

The word **immoral** means 'wrong'. An immoral act is an action that is thought to be morally wrong. This means that it is an unacceptable way to behave.

The word **amoral** means 'without moral standards or principles'. Someone who is amoral shows no understanding of what is right or wrong.

How do Christians decide what is right and wrong?

Christians try to live their lives in the way they think God wants. They believe that God sent Jesus to show them the right way to live. When making a moral decision, many Christians would ask 'what would Jesus do in this situation?' and try to follow his example. Jesus' life and teachings are the main source of moral authority for most Christians. A source of authority is something or someone which tells a person what to do.

Christians can find out what Jesus might have done by reading the **Gospels** in the Bible. The Bible also contains laws and other information about the right way to live such as the Ten Commandments and the words of the **prophets**. Using the Bible as a source of authority can sometimes be difficult for Christians. This is because the world in which the writers of the Bible and Jesus lived was very different to the world today. The issues modern Christians have to face may not be mentioned specifically in the Bible. In some situations, the Bible can only act as a guide and Christians must think things through carefully themselves and follow their own conscience. Christians might also look at what the official teachings of their Church say about an issue and ask the advice of other Christians.

Animal rights

Christians believe that animals are an important part of God's creation but they have different views about how animals should be treated. Most Christians think that animals do not have the same rights as human beings but they should still be treated with kindness and respect. Many Christians disagree with 'blood sports', intensive farming methods and using animals for toiletries and cosmetic testing. Some Christians, however, accept that using animals to test the safety of medicines and chemicals and to improve veterinary knowledge can be helpful.

Wolves and sheep will live together in peace and leopards will lie down with young goats.
Calves and lion cubs will feed together,
and little children will take care of them.
Cows and bears will eat together,
and their calves and cubs will lie down in peace.
Lions will eat straw as cattle do.
Even a baby will not be harmed
if it plays near a poisonous snake.

Isaiah 11: 6–8

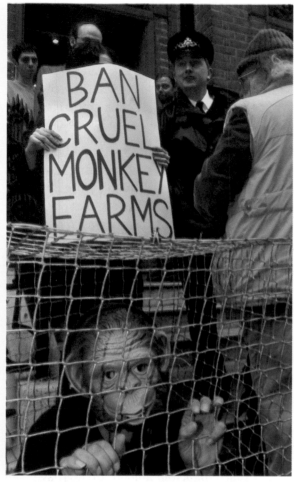

An animal rights protest against Spanish monkey farms

Other Christians say that human beings should live in harmony with animals and not exploit them in any way whatsoever. The Religious Society of Friends, Quakers, have always been very concerned about the rights of animals. A large number of Christians who belong to this denomination are vegetarians. Most Quakers would also disagree with fur coats, circuses which use animals and zoos.

Christians founded the RSPCA and there are other Christian organizations which work to protect the rights of animals. A lady called May Tripp set up the Animal Christian Concern (ACC) society. She noticed that her dog had his own unique personality and needs. One day when he was in pain May thought about how animals being hunted or experimented on suffered and she decided to do something to protect them.

The ACC encourages Christians and non-Christians to get involved in animal welfare issues. Another part of their work includes organizing church services where worshippers pray for suffering animals. Some churches allow pets to attend these services This idea is based on a verse in the Bible, Ephesians 1: 10, which says that all of creation should come together to worship God.

Learning about religion

❶ Think of a moral issue that is important today. Draw a flow chart showing the process Christians might go through when making a decision about it. What sources of moral authority might influence their decision-making?

❷ Read the story of Noah's Ark in Genesis 6: 9 – 9: 17 in the Old Testament. Explain how you think this story might help Christians come to a decision about the treatment of animals.

❸ 'Churches are for humans not animals.' Do you agree? Explain your reasons, providing examples to support your arguments.

Learning from religion

❶ Write your own Ten Commandments for people to follow.

❷ How do you decide what is right and wrong? Draw a diagram which shows your main sources of moral authority.

❸ Prepare a speech to present to the rest of your class about your views on animal rights, giving examples to support your statements.

Moral issues 2

In this section you will:

- find how Christians believe people should treat each other

- learn about the Christian attitude towards prejudice and discrimination

- have the opportunity to express your own views on these issues.

Prejudice is when you prejudge someone. This means that you form an opinion about them without knowing what they are like.
Discrimination is when you act on your prejudice and treat some people better or worse than other people because of what you believe to be true about them. There are many different kinds of prejudice and people can be discriminated against for a variety of reasons such as size, accent, colour of skin, gender, age, ability and race. Discrimination on the basis of race or colour of skin is known as racism. Treating people the same way regardless of their status, physical characteristics or mental abilities is called equality.

Prejudice can lead to stereotyping. This is when you form fixed mental images about what a particular group of people are like. Stereotyping assumes that every member of a group is the same and will act the same way.

Christian teachings disagree with prejudice and discrimination. They say that everyone is created and loved by God and should therefore be treated equally. Christians believe that one of the reasons Jesus came to Earth was to put an end to prejudice and discrimination.

According to the Bible, Jesus did not discriminate against anyone. He told his followers that they must treat other people as they would like to be treated themselves. This is known as the Golden Rule. Jesus taught that part of loving God included loving their neighbour as themselves. Using the **parable** of the Good Samaritan, found in Luke 10: 25–37 in the **New Testament**, Jesus explained that the term 'neighbour' meant everyone, particularly people in need. The kind of love Christians must try and show to others is called **agape**.

Agape is an unconditional and self-sacrificing love. It involves putting yourself out to help others and expecting nothing in return.

'…God treats everyone on the same basis.'

(Acts 10: 24)

'…From one human being [God] created all races on earth and made them live, throughout the whole earth.'

(Acts 17: 26)

'…there is no difference between Jews and Gentiles, between slaves and free men, between men and women; you are all one in union with Christ Jesus.'

(Galatians 3: 28)

How have Christians responded to prejudice and discrimination?

Dr Martin Luther King

Dr Martin Luther King, a black American civil rights leader, fought for the equal treatment of black and white people in the Southern States of America, using non-violent forms of protest. He was assassinated in 1968.

'…I have a dream that my four little children will one day live in a nation where they will not be judged by the colour of their skin but by the content of their character…'

Dr Martin Luther King

Nelson Mandela

Nelson Mandela, a black South African leader, was imprisoned for 28 years for his opposition to **apartheid**, a system of racial segregation in South Africa. He was released from prison in 1990 and continues to work for the equal treatment of black people in South Africa.

'…Let there be justice for all. Let there be peace for all. Let there be work, bread, water and salt for all…'

Nelson Mandela

Mother Teresa

Many Christians believe that Mother Teresa is a good example of agape love

Mother Teresa, a Roman Catholic nun, devoted her life to caring for the 'poorest of the poor' in India. She fought against poverty and disease and helped people regardless of their race or religion.

'There is only one God and He is God to all; therefore it is important that everyone is seen as equal before God.'
I've always said we should help a Hindu become a better Hindu, a Muslim become a better Muslim, a Catholic become a better Catholic.'

Mother Teresa

Learning about religion

❶ Design a symbol and slogan which Christians could use to demonstrate what their faith teaches about prejudice and discrimination.

❷ 'One good turn deserves another.' How do you think Christians might respond to this statement? Give reasons for your answer.

❸ In groups, find out more about the Christians mentioned on this page and evaluate the contributions they have made to racial equality and harmony and the role faith has played in their work.

Learning from religion

❶ Explain what your Golden Rule would be and why.

❷ Imagine that you are in charge of Equal Opportunities at your school. What could you do to make sure that everyone is treated equally?

❸ 'We were all made different for a reason.' Do you agree? Discuss this statement in groups.

Ultimate questions 1

In this section you will:

- explore some Christian responses to ultimate questions
- have the opportunity to think about how the existence of God could help to explain some of life's mysteries
- be able to express your own views on why we exist and the purpose and meaning of life.

What is an ultimate question?

Ultimate questions are very important questions to which there are no definite or absolute answers, like 'Does God exist?' or 'How did everything begin?' They are usually questions about something in life which is difficult to understand, explain or prove. People often ask ultimate questions to try and make sense of the world in which they live. They also ask ultimate questions to find purpose and meaning in their lives. There are many things in life that cannot easily be explained and the way people respond to or answer ultimate questions depends on their beliefs. Many people believe that the existence of God can explain these mysteries. Christianity, like other religions, has beliefs which try to provide answers to ultimate questions or give people hope that there may be answers to them.

Christians believe that all life is a precious gift from God. They say that we exist because God has chosen to give us life. Christians believe that every individual is unique and special because they are created, known and loved by God. The idea that all life is sacred because it comes from God is called the **sanctity of life** . The Christian belief in the sanctity of life affects how they deal with issues such as genetic engineering, embryo technology, abortion and euthanasia.

What are we here for?

'My commandment is this: love one another as I have loved you.' (John 15: 12)

Why do we exist?

'Then God said, "And now we will make human beings; they will be like us and resemble us…" So God created human beings, making them to be like himself. He created them male and female…'

Genesis 1: 26–7

Christians believe that God created human beings for a reason. They say that life on earth is part of God's plan for human beings. Christians believe that human beings were made to have a personal relationship with God which begins in this life and continues after death. They claim that life on Earth gives human beings the opportunity to get to know God and develop their relationship with Him. Christians say that their purpose in life is to love and serve God. This involves helping and caring for other people, as Christians believe that all human beings are made in the 'image' of God. They take this to mean that people have godlike characteristics and should therefore be valued and respected, not that they are exactly like God.

'The dying, the cripple, the mental, the unwanted, the unloved – they are all Jesus in disguise.'

Mother Teresa

What happens when we die?

Christians believe that life is eternal. This means that it continues after death. Christians think that the soul, a person's spirit, lives on after death.

They believe that human beings are given life by God in the beginning and have the opportunity to be with God when they die. Christians claim that what happens to us after death depends on how we have lived our lives on Earth. If we have led a good life we will be in the presence of God and experience a state known as Heaven. If we have led a bad life we will be apart from God and experience a state known as Hell. Some Christians argue that not many people can hope to enter Heaven straight away. Roman Catholics believe that most people go through another stage of preparation called '**purgatory**'.

Learning about religion

❶ In groups, find out how other religions might respond to questions about why we exist and the meaning and purpose of life. Compare and contrast your findings with Christianity.

❷ Explain why you think religious people might argue that the existence of God helps to explain some of life's mysteries.

❸ Describe what you think it might feel like to be in the presence of God.

Learning from religion

❶ What ultimate question would you most like to know the answer to and why?

❷ Explain why you think we exist and what you believe is the purpose and meaning of life.

❸ 'Sometimes there are no answers just more questions.' Discuss in pairs what you think this statement means.

Ultimate questions 2

In this section you will:

● look at how Christians respond to the problems of evil and suffering

● have the opportunity to reflect upon some of the issues raised such as the existence of God and the origins of evil.

Flooding in the United Kingdom

Why do people suffer?

One of the most difficult questions to answer is 'why do people suffer?' It is a particularly difficult question to answer if, like **Christians**, you believe in an all-loving, all-powerful and all-knowing God. Many people argue that there is so much suffering in the world that God cannot possibly exist. They say that if God did exist He or She would not allow human beings to suffer. Other people say that even if God does exist the large amount of suffering in the world means that God's powers are limited in some way. Some people also say that suffering is a fact of life. It is part of what it means to be human and without God's help and support life would sometimes be unbearable.

People's ideas and beliefs about suffering can also change according to their experiences. For religious people, personal suffering is often a test of faith. Some lose their faith and turn away from God whilst others claim that the difficult experiences in their lives have made them better people, strengthened their faith and brought them closer to God. There are also people who have become religious as a result of their suffering.

'My faith died along with my daughter. I gave her a Christian burial because everyone expected that of me but as I stood at her graveside I thought this is pointless. There is no God.'

'I was christened as a baby but I never really thought about God at all until I became ill with cancer. One day when I was feeling depressed and unhappy, a friend of mine, who is a Christian, persuaded me to go to church with her. I came out of the service feeling a sense of peace and I felt hopeful about my life. I went to church regularly after that and I've recently decided to get confirmed.'

Where does suffering come from?

There are many different causes of suffering. Sometimes suffering occurs as a result of a natural disaster such as an earthquake or flooding. It is described as natural because it does not seem to result from human action.

The devastation caused by an earthquake in India

Suffering can also be caused by human beings through deliberate acts of violence such as murder, terrorism and war. This kind of suffering is the result of human-made or moral evil. The word 'evil' means 'wrong or wicked'. We say something is evil when it causes harm or injury to people.

Not all causes of suffering fit into these two categories. For example, human beings sometimes cause suffering to others accidentally and some natural disasters are the result of humans misusing or abusing natural resources.

What is the Christian response to suffering?

The Christian writer C. S. Lewis (author of the *Chronicles of Narnia*) once said that 'pain was God's megaphone for rousing a deaf world'. He thought that pain and suffering was God's way of getting people to turn to him. C. S. Lewis also likened God to a sculptor trying to create a perfect statue. He said that pain and suffering was God's chisel, His way of making us become better people.

Christians have different ideas and beliefs about why people suffer and what the presence of suffering in the world means. Most Christians believe that the majority of suffering in the world is caused by human sin. They believe that when God created human beings he gave them **free will**. This means that they are able to choose how to behave. When human beings turn away from God and do evil things it results in suffering. Some Christians believe that there is a supernatural evil force called the Devil (Satan) which encourages human beings to do wicked things. They believe that the Devil is responsible for all the evil in the world.

Other Christians see suffering as kind of test. They get this idea from a book in the Bible called Job which tells the story of a man who is tested by suffering to see if he will continue to worship, praise and believe in God. Another view is that you shouldn't question God about suffering.

You just have to trust that God knows what He or She is doing. There is also the idea that you will be rewarded after death for the suffering you experience on Earth.

Most Christians believe that God understands suffering and pain. They say that by becoming a man in Jesus God knows what it is like to suffer. Christians are taught that they should keep worshipping, praising and believing in God no matter what happens.

Learning about religion

❶ Explain why you think Christians believe that God understands suffering and pain.

❷ 'Suffering is good for the soul.' What do you think this statement means and how does it relate to Christian ideas about suffering?

❸ Make a list of the reasons why people might continue to believe in God despite the existence of evil and suffering.

Learning from religion

❶ Discuss in groups the different ways people can suffer and decide whether they are caused by natural phenomena or human-made evil.

❷ Explain why you think suffering and evil exist.

❸ In pairs, produce a plan of action which outlines what human beings could do to reduce the amount of suffering and evil in the world.

Glossary

Agape unconditional, self-sacrificing, non-romantic love which Christians believe they should try and demonstrate to others

Amoral without moral qualities, characteristics

Anointed being smeared with consecrated oil

Anointing of the Sick being anointed with holy oil during some ceremonies

Apartheid a system of racial segregation in South Africa

Apocrypha (from a Greek word meaning 'hidden') a collection of seven books which the Roman Catholic Church accepts as part of its scriptures

Apostles (from the Greek word 'to send') the name given to the original twelve disciples of Jesus. Christians believe they were 'sent out' into the world by God to tell people about Jesus

Apparition the appearance of a supernatural figure

Ascension the belief that Jesus went up (ascended) into the presence of God (Heaven)

Atonement the idea of being 'at one' or reconciled with God through the death of Jesus

Baptism the ceremony by which some people become members of the Christian Church

Baptistry a small pool containing enough water for a person to be fully immersed during a baptism ceremony

Believers' baptism a ceremony by which young people or adults become full members of the Christian Church

Blasphemy being disrespectful to God

Chrismation a ceremony carried out straight after baptism in the Orthodox Church

Christ the name given to Jesus by his followers after his death when they believed he had been resurrected

Christians the name given to the followers of the Christ (Jesus)

Church the name given to the building in which Christians worship; different denominations within Christianity; the worldwide Christian community

Clergy a group of people who are ordained and authorized to lead worship and look after the congregation of a church in a Christian denomination

Confession the act of admitting to God, through a priest, what one has done wrong and expressing sorrow and regret for it

Confirmation the ceremony where Christians publicly confirm the vows made on their behalf at baptism and become full or grown up members of the Christian Church

Congregation a group of people who have gathered together for worship

Consecrated holy, blessed, set apart; something which is made holy and set aside for religious purposes

Creed (from the Latin word *credo* meaning 'I believe') a statement of belief

Crematorium a building in which corpses are cremated

Cross the symbol of Christianity

Crucifix a particular kind of cross which has an image of Jesus on it

Denomination a separate Christian group which shares the same name and beliefs

Disciples followers of Jesus including the twelve men Jesus chose especially to help him carry out his work on earth

Discrimination the action taken as a result of prejudice

Divine godlike

Easter Day the day Christians celebrate their belief in Jesus' resurrection, one of the most joyful and happy days in the Christian year

Ecumenical belonging to the 'world-wide' Christian Church

Episcopal (from the Greek word meaning 'bishop') a term used to describe a Church which has bishops

Epistles long and usually quite formal letters containing Christian teachings

Eternal life the belief that life continues after death

Eucharist the name given to a service of Holy Communion; it means 'thanksgiving'

Evolution the gradual and natural development of the universe over a long period of time

Forgiveness to forgive or be forgiven, to stop thinking badly of someone or no longer be thought of badly because of wrongdoings

Free will the idea that God has given human beings the freedom to choose how to behave

Genuflection a series of movements made during worship which show respect for God

Good Friday the day on which Christians remember Jesus' death

Gospels (from a Greek word meaning 'good news') the first four books of the New Testament: Matthew, Mark, Luke and John. These tell the story of Jesus and his teachings

Great Schism the split of the Christian Church into two parts, the Catholic Church and the Orthodox Church, in 1054

Hebrew the language of the Jewish people

Heresy a belief which is different to the official teachings of the Christian Church

Holy associated with God, sacred

Holy Communion a church service during which Christians share bread and wine together in memory of Jesus; the act of receiving bread and wine during the Eucharist

Holy Saturday the last day of Lent, the day before Easter Day, when Christians get ready to celebrate their belief in Jesus' resurrection

Holy Spirit the third person of the Trinity, an invisible divine power which guides and inspires human beings

Holy water water which has been blessed and put aside for holy purposes such as baptism

Holy Week the period in the Christian year when Christians focus on the events associated with the death and resurrection of Jesus

Humility being humble, showing that you recognize your failings and weaknesses

Immoral unacceptable, wrong behaviour

Incarnation the act of God becoming a human being in Jesus

Incense a sweet smelling substance which gives off an odour when burnt

Infant baptism a ceremony by which children are welcomed into the Christian Church

Interfaith involving different religions

Laity ordinary members of a Christian congregation who have not been ordained

Last Supper the name given to the final meal Jesus shared with his disciples

Lectionary a book containing an ordered set of Bible readings for Christians to study at set times throughout the year

Liturgy (from a Greek word meaning 'service') set form of service used by a church

Marriage the religious or legal ceremony by which people become 'man and wife'

Martyrs people who suffer or die for their beliefs

Maundy Thursday the day before Good Friday when Christians remember the final meal or Last Supper Jesus had with his disciples

Meditation a form of quiet prayer which involves clearing the mind of all distractions and concentrating on God

Messiah (Mashiah) Hebrew word meaning the 'Anointed One', a saviour sent from God

Midnight Mass special service held late at night on Christmas Eve to commemorate the birth of Jesus

Ministry time spent in the service of God

Missionaries people who are sent to places by their church to spread the Christian faith.

Moral conforming to accepted good standards of general behaviour

New Testament a collection of Christian writings which include the Gospels

Old Testament the Christian name for the Jewish scriptures, the first part of the Christian Bible

Ordination the service by which a person becomes a priest

Pacifists people who disagree with the use of violence

Pagan an ancient religion based on the natural world

Palm Sunday the day Christians commemorate Jesus arriving in Jerusalem on a donkey shortly before he was crucified. It is the last Sunday of Lent and the first day of Holy Week

Parable a short story which makes a religious or moral point

Paschal candle a large candle which is lit in many churches on Holy Saturday to represent the light of Jesus

Penance a voluntary act to make up or atone for wrongdoings

Pesach (Passover) Jewish festival which reminds the Jews of how God rescued them from slavery in Egypt

Pilgrim the name given to someone who goes on a religious journey or pilgrimage

Pilgrimage a religious journey

Pope the leader of the Roman Catholic Church

Prayer a way of approaching or communicating with God

Prejudice to prejudge someone for no good reason

Priest the title given to people who have been ordained and are authorized to lead worship and look after the congregation in the Anglican, Roman Catholic and Orthodox Churches. Priests are also known as vicars in the Church of England

Prophets important people in the Bible who are believed to have been inspired by God

Protestant (from the word 'protest') the name given to the new Churches which were formed as a result of the Reformation

Psalms a collection of 150 religious songs, poems and prayers which are sung or chanted during Christian services or ceremonies

Purgatory according to Roman Catholic belief, a state after death where the soul is purified and made ready to go to Heaven

Reconciliation the idea that Jesus' death repaired the relationship between God and human beings and brought them together

Redeemer a title Christians have given to Jesus because they believe he rescued or freed people from the consequences of their sins

Redemption the idea of Jesus saving human beings from the consequences of their sins

Reformation a religious revolution in the Catholic Church during the sixteenth century

Repentance showing regret for wrongdoings, turning away from sin and living the way God wants

Resurrection the belief that Jesus rose from the dead and overcame death

Revelation God revealing or making Himself/Herself known to human beings

Rites of passage rituals which mark important human experiences such as baptism, confirmation, marriage and death

Sacrament a sacred experience or event where Christians believe they receive special blessings from God

Saint someone who has been recognized after their death as being especially holy and dedicated to God whilst they were alive

Salvation being saved from sin, having a personal relationship with God

Salvation Army a Protestant denomination founded by William Booth in 1865, which is organized in a military way and has its own uniform

Sanctity of life the idea that all life is precious and sacred because it is a gift from God

Saviour a person who has saved someone. This is a title Christians have given Jesus because they believe he saved people from the consequences of their sins

Scriptures writings inspired by God

Second Coming the belief that Jesus will return to Earth one day to finally judge human beings

Secular non-religious

Sermon the part of the service when the priest talks to the congregation about some aspect of Christian belief and practice

Shrine a special area associated with a holy person or object

Sins thoughts or actions that go against the will of God

Stewardship the idea that human beings have a responsibility to look after the earth

Tenakh Jewish name for the Old Testament

Transubstantiation the belief that the bread and wine actually became the body and blood of Jesus Christ during the Eucharist

Trinity the belief that there are three persons within the one God: God the Father, God the Son and God the Holy Spirit

Vestments special clothing worn by members of the clergy when they take part in worship

Virgin Mary a title given to Mary the mother of Jesus which reflects the Christian belief that she was a pure and good person

Index